Contents

	1. Audit	2. Feedback
About the series		5
About this book		5
Introduction	6	40
Task A: Mutiplication and division	8	42
Task B: Fractions	12	46
Task C: Generalized arithmetic	16	51
Task D: Pattern and proof	20	56
Task E: Equations and graphs	24	60
Task F: Geometry	28	64
Task G: Properties of shapes	32	69
Task H: Statistics and probability	36	74

		3. Key ideas
The nature of maths		80
Algebra		84
Proof		86
Keep the value: change the appearance		88
The language of maths		90
Glossary		92
Further reading		94
Personal learning plan		95

Mathematics for Primary Teachers

An Audit and Self-Study Guide

Sue Jennings and Richard Dunne

EDUCATIONAL

Aldine Place
London
W12 8AW

Tel: 0181-740 2266
Fax: 0181-743 8451

Acknowledgements

The publishers and authors would like to thank the Teacher Training Agency – in particular Frankie Sulke and Annie Grant for their constructive comments on these materials. Much of the content has been stimulated by, and draws on, national initiatives undertaken in part by the authors on behalf of the TTA and other agencies concerned with standards, oracy, literacy and numeracy. Thanks are due to the staff at University of Exeter School of Education, Homerton College Cambridge, Westhill College Birmingham and the University of Wolverhampton, particularly Christine Doddington, Gill Hackett, Charmaine Hebbard, Anne Thwaites, Keith Warburton, Nigel Woodhead and Roger Woods. Special thanks to Roger Trend in the School of Education, Exeter, for co-ordinating the new QTS series, to Barry Sutcliffe at Topics for project management above and beyond the call of duty, and to Chris Kington of Chris Kington Publishing without whose help and dedication the project would never have been completed.

A CIP catalogue record is available from the British Library

ISBN 1-85805-316-1
Copyright Sue Jennings and Richard Dunne © 1997

Reprinted 1997

Designed and edited by Topics – The Creative Partnership, Exeter

Printed and bound in Great Britain by Livesey Ltd, Shrewsbury

The Letts QTS Series offers support for all those preparing to become teachers and working towards Qualified Teacher Status (QTS). The content, teaching approaches and practical ideas are useful for trainee teachers, teacher tutors and mentors, and teacher educators in higher education.

The Letts QTS Series addresses the new standards for QTS and the content of the Initial Teacher Training National Curriculum (ITTNC). These are central to the improvement of standards in schools. The series is specifically designed to help all trainee teachers cover the content of the ITTNC and achieve the national standards in order to be awarded QTS.

The short series handbook *QTS: A Practical Introduction* gives trainees an overview of the QTS requirement and a more detailed interpretation of each standard.

The other books in the Letts QTS Series offer trainees the chance to audit their knowledge of the content of the subjects in the ITTNC, pinpoint areas of further work, and use support materials to develop their knowledge. The first two subjects addressed are English and Mathematics for primary teachers.

There are two Letts QTS Series books for each subject:

Book 1 addresses trainees' subject knowledge at their own level by offering a systematic and comprehensive guide to the subject knowledge requirements of the ITTNC. Trainees can check their own knowledge of the subject against that specified in the ITTNC. Section one provides a comprehensive **audit** of this subject knowledge and understanding, with helpful **feedback** and follow-up set out in section two. Having identified areas of subject knowledge for attention, trainees can then use the support materials in section three to develop **key ideas** and map out their **personal learning plan**.

Book 2 for each subject is a handbook of **lesson plans**, **knowledge** and **methods**. This provides details of carefully selected lessons which illustrate effective teaching. It shows how lesson planning and classroom teaching draw on a high level of subject knowledge. It demonstrates how carefully integrated whole-class teaching and group and individual work can be designed to ensure that pupils make progress in their learning.

There is also a tutor-support pack for each subject.

The Letts QTS Series aims to break down the requirements of QTS into manageable units so that trainees can evaluate and improve their knowledge of each subject. The books in the series are written in a straightforward way by authors who are all experienced teachers, teacher educators, researchers, writers and specialists in their subject areas.

Titles on Information Technology and Science for primary teachers will follow, together with titles for trainees preparing to teach in the secondary phase of schooling.

This book is for everyone who wants to learn maths in order to teach in a primary school. There are three main sections:

Audit
Feedback
Key ideas

The *Audit* contains maths questions organized as eight tasks. This is not a test. It provides an outline of what you need to know to teach maths so that you can assess your needs and plan your work. You get help with this by using the *Feedback*. This contains answers to the questions in the *Audit* but it has a second equally important role. The *Feedback* provides you with a picture of how you need to know maths in order to teach it.

You need to know rather a lot about how different topics in maths relate to each other and you need to be confident and accurate in your use of language. The structure of the book helps you with this. Each page has three columns. The centre column contains the main text. The left-hand column carries a quick summary of the main text. The right-hand column gives hints and related comments as well as directing you to other sections in the book.

Maths can seem a rather difficult subject. When people find it hard it is usually because they have not been helped to see the connections between seemingly separate topics. They do not have an overview. They have not been let into the secret. But there is an essential coherence in maths. There are relatively few big ideas that hold the key to understanding. We have summarized these in the third section, *Key ideas*. You will need to read this section patiently, thoroughly and many times. You will need to carry in your head the main thrust of each key idea. At the very least you will need to recall their titles instinctively. You could turn to this section now and get your first taste of the five *Key ideas*:

The nature of maths
Algebra
Proof
Keep the value: change the appearance
The language of maths

Remember that this book is about planning your learning of maths. The *Personal learning plan* provides a way of recording your planning and monitoring your progress. As you study the questions in the audit and the appropriate feedback you will need to record what you have achieved and what needs doing. You will need to evaluate the resources available to you (forthcoming lectures; access to tutors) and plan your attack. Record this in the *Personal learning plan*. Periodically review what impact you are making and modify your plan. In short: take charge.

Audit

What is meant by an audit?

An audit is not a test. When you audit your knowledge and performance you make a professional and dispassionate assessment of your achievements and your needs. The foremost purpose of this is so that you can plan future work to meet your needs.

You do not simply have needs. You have needs in relation to something. This book is for everyone who wants to achieve a level of mathematical understanding, knowledge and skill in order to teach. The purpose of the audit is to provide an outline of what it means to know maths appropriate for teaching.

The audit in this book contains maths questions. You will probably soon spot one that you cannot do. When this happens you will need some immediate assistance to be able to do it. This is the purpose of the *Feedback* section. You may find that when you see the feedback (maybe just the answer; maybe the advice) you will say 'If I had known that was what was wanted I could have done it'. Fine. You have learnt what it means to do a question of that type. Perhaps the feedback will not clarify things. You may find that a friend or colleague will be able to help. You may need to consult a tutor. The point is that the audit does not take place under exam conditions. It is to enable you to learn.

This style of coming to know something is especially important for teaching. You are not expected to memorize and instantly recall everything in the audit. But you must achieve sufficient familiarity with the material to be able to read and make sense of the sort of help provided by the feedback.

What does the audit cover?

The maths that appears in this audit is largely the topics you will have covered before, although it is likely that it will be more rigorous. There is an emphasis on correct terminology that may not have been of paramount importance in your previous contact with maths. The accuracy and the rigour are important because teachers must know what lies beneath a problem rather than merely grope for a solution that meets with the approval of others. There is a special emphasis in the audit on how algebraic structures underpin arithmetic.

The audit covers the maths that you need to know. You cannot treat the content in the way that you may have done in a test: 'Although I could not do any of that section I got full marks in this one so I was O.K.' There is no room for compensation of this sort. You have a special responsibility to know.

What is the content of the audit?

The audit consists of eight tasks designed to enable you to make links and connections between seemingly separate areas of maths. The tasks are designed on the assumption that you have studied maths successfully to the equivalent of at least GCSE grade C.

How should you use the audit?

You should use the audit in conjunction with the feedback. We would expect you to have the audit open at a particular task and to have a marker at the appropriate point in the feedback so you can flip between them. We would expect to see you periodically rereading the *Key ideas* section during the course of tackling a question.

You will in all likelihood work closely with others so that you can regularly discuss difficulties and describe successes. You will have easy access to maths text books and you will plan contact with tutors to capitalize fully on their expertise. Above all you will be working confidently with a happy smile on your face!

How can you make best use of the columns in the audit?

The notes in the left-hand column give you a quick summary of what is in the task. You should study these from time to time and ask yourself 'Does this phrase summarize what I am getting from this question?' The notes in the right-hand column give advice and other related comments and direct you to other sections in this book. You should follow up these cross references. In particular you ought to pursue the references to the *Key ideas* section because they will gradually strengthen your grasp of the essential coherence of maths.

How does the audit work with the personal learning plan?

Study the *Personal learning plan* at the end of this book. As you work through the tasks maintain a record of your successes and your needs. It doesn't matter if you struggled with the task at first if you feel confident after referring to the feedback. This is success. Record it.

What sort of action should you take to follow up the audit?

Your work with the audit and your notes in the *Personal learning plan* will record your progress. But problems will remain. Analyse them. Try to go beyond 'I just do not get it' to see if you can specify what causes the problem. Remember that these blocks happen with all of us at all stages of learning. You are normal. Study the programme for your course to see where you will be receiving instruction in this topic. Plan for a tutorial. Be entirely open about what you find difficult. Refer specifically to the item in the audit. Talk through the feedback that has not yet helped you. Persist in your search for clarification. Remember that whenever you describe your confusion there will be any number of people near you wishing they had had the courage to be as open as you.

Task A: Multiplication and division

When you multiply large numbers it is sensible to use a calculator but you also need to know mental or written methods. There are elegant and efficient strategies which depend on the methods and algebraic laws that underpin arithmetic. These can be taught. You will see that the advantage of using them is that knowing how to achieve one answer can help you with many other calculations. The questions below tease out the underpinning ideas and test your number fluency.

Approximation

A1

(a) When dealing with any numerical problem it is useful to have some idea of the answer before doing the calculation. Write down a reasonable approximation for 43×27.

Long multiplication

(b) Examine each of the four ways of laying out a long multiplication shown below and explain why each is correct.

> You should be able to refer to the commutative and distributive laws here. If you need help look them up in *Key ideas: The nature of maths*.

$$
\begin{array}{r} 43 \\ \times 27 \\ \hline 860 \\ 301 \\ \hline 1161 \end{array}
\qquad
\begin{array}{r} 43 \\ \times 27 \\ \hline 301 \\ 860 \\ \hline 1161 \end{array}
\qquad
\begin{array}{r} 27 \\ \times 43 \\ \hline 1080 \\ 81 \\ \hline 1161 \end{array}
\qquad
\begin{array}{r} 27 \\ \times 43 \\ \hline 81 \\ 1080 \\ \hline 1161 \end{array}
$$

A2

This is another way of setting out the same multiplication:

> This way of setting out multiplication is particularly helpful in providing a basis for later work in algebra. See *Audit: Task D*.

×	40		3		
20	800		60		860
7	280		21		301
					1161

The distributive law

Show how this is related to the distributive law by completing the following:

$$(40 + 3) \times (20 + 7) =$$

Using mental methods

A3

Each of the following calculations is related in some way to 43×27. Use the fact that $43 \times 27 = 1161$ to write down the answers without doing any written calculations and without using a calculator.

> In parts (k) to (n) the numbers are written in standard form. Use the feedback if you have forgotten how to do these.

(a) 27×43

(b) 43×2.7

(c) 27×4.3

(d) 4.3×2.7

(e) $4\frac{3}{10} \times 2\frac{7}{10}$

(f) $\frac{43}{1000} \times \frac{27}{100}$

(g) 27000×430

(h) 4300×270

(i) $4.3 \times {}^-2.7$

(j) $^-2.7 \times {}^-0.43$

(k) $4.3 \times 10^7 \times 2.7 \times 10^9$

(l) $2.7 \times 10^4 \times 4.3 \times 10^{-6}$

(m) $2.7 \times 10^{-4} \times 4.3 \times 10^{-3}$

(n) $4.3 \times 10^a \times 2.7 \times 10^b$

A4

We often need to multiply two numbers when calculating areas and volumes. In this question you will focus on the mathematical processes involved and the appropriateness of the answer.

(a)

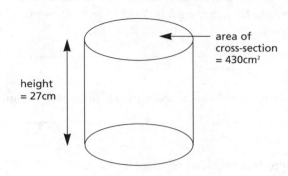

Volume of a cylinder

The area of cross-section of this cylinder is 430cm² and its perpendicular height is 27cm. Work out the volume of the cylinder.

> You can find the formulae for the volumes of solids in the *Glossary*.

(b)

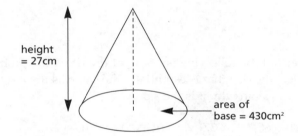

Relationship between the volume of a cylinder and the volume of a cone

The area of the circular base of this cone is 430cm² and its perpendicular height is 27cm. Use your answer to (a) to work out the volume of the cone.

(c)

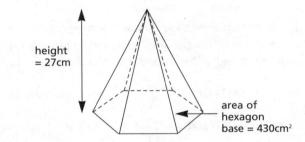

Relationship between the volume of a pyramid and those of cones and cylinders

The area of the hexagonal base of this pyramid is 430cm² and its perpendicular height is 27cm. How does its volume relate to the volumes of (a) and (b) respectively?

....

A5

Using and applying mathematics

This question illustrates how multiplication can be applied to word problems.

Four hundred and thirty children in a school each use on average nine exercise books a year. How many books is this altogether?

> 'How many' can trigger multiplication or division. You have to look for other words to decide which is applicable.

Most methods for the division of one number by another look complicated. When the numbers involved are large, you are well advised to use a calculator but (as with multiplication) you become more fluent with numbers in general when you understand how the division process works. The algorithm for long division offers an excellent foundation for later work in algebra as well as practice in basic number work.

> Use the *Glossary* to look up the word 'algorithm'.

A6

Is division commutative? Give an example to illustrate your answer.

Long division

A7

This is the traditional long division algorithm:

$$
\begin{array}{r}
43 \\
27\,\overline{)\,1161} \\
108 \\
\hline
81 \\
81 \\
\hline
00
\end{array}
$$

Check that each of the following is a way of rewriting the problem $1161 \div 27$. Select the one that is essentially the same as the long division algorithm and explain why it is the same.

(a) $(1000 + 100 + 60 + 1) \div 27$ (d) $(1000 + 161) \div 27$

(b) $(1100 + 61) \div 27$ (e) $(270 + 270 + 270 + 270 + 81) \div 27$

(c) $(1080 + 81) \div 27$ (f) $(540 + 540 + 27 + 27 + 27) \div 27$

> See how in all of these examples we 'keep the value but change the appearance'. This is a particularly powerful idea in mathematics. See *Key ideas* for more on this.

Using mental methods

A8

Each of the following calculations is related in some way to the result $43 \times 27 = 1161$. Use this fact to write down the answers without doing any written calculations and without using a calculator.

(a) $1161 \div 43$ (d) $116.1 \div 2.7$ (g) $11\frac{61}{100} \div 2\frac{7}{10}$

(b) $1161 \div 2.7$ (e) $116100 \div 430$ (h) $1.161 \times 10^9 \div 4.3 \times 10^5$

(c) $11.61 \div 43$ (f) $1.161 \div 0.027$

Using and applying mathematics

A9

It is important to recognize when a word problem invites the division process. Answer each of the following and make notes about words or phrases that trigger the thought 'Ah! It's division'.

(a) £116.10 was shared equally amongst 430 children. How much did each child get?

(b) One thousand one hundred and sixty-one pennies were put in piles of nine pence each. How many piles were there?

> Division can be confusing because sometimes we are asking 'how many of...?' and other times 'how many groups of...?'

Mathematical processes

A10

We often need to divide two numbers when calculating areas and volumes. In this question (as with the earlier one for multiplication) you will focus on the mathematical processes involved and the appropriateness of the answer.

(a)

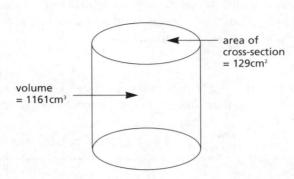

> Look in the *Glossary* for the formulae for volumes of solids.

The volume of this cylinder is 1161cm³ and its circular cross-section is 129cm². Work out its perpendicular height.

(b)

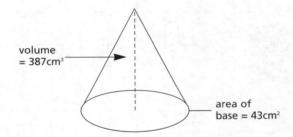

The volume of this cone is 387cm³ and the area of its circular base is 43cm². Work out its perpendicular height.

(c)

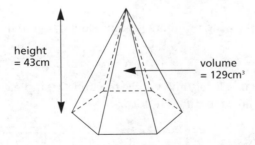

> The answer to this question should prompt you to check the measurements given. It may be that for a given context the dimensions are appropriate.

Checking for sensible answers

The volume of this hexagonal-based pyramid is 129cm³ and its perpendicular height is 43cm. Work out the area of its hexagonal base.

A11

The sum of the lengths of the edges of a cube is 96cm. What is the length of an edge of this cube?

Task B: Fractions

Check the feedback if you do not know these terms.

Confusion about fractions is widespread. For many people, fractions seem to be governed by a set of strange rules unrelated to anything else. This is a serious problem. This task emphasizes how different forms of fractions are closely related. If you are able to think about vulgar fractions, decimal fractions, percentages, ratio and scale factor as a single idea then you can understand all of them better.

Different forms for fractions

See *Key ideas: Keep the value: change the appearance* in this book and *Lessons: Fractions* in Book 2.

B1

Fractions are used in many different forms. Look at the numbers that appear in the first row in the table and tick the boxes which describe the *form* of the number.

	$\frac{1}{5}$	$\frac{7}{3}$	0.3	$0.\dot{3}$	10%	1:4	$0.6\dot{7}$	67%	1:17	0.317
vulgar fraction										
proper fraction										
improper fraction										
decimal fraction										
finite decimal fraction										
infinite recurring decimal fraction										
percentage										
ratio										

Equivalence

B2

Equivalence is an important concept in mathematics. This question looks at equivalence in value.

(a) Which of the following numbers is equivalent in value to a third?

$$\frac{2}{6} \quad 0.3 \quad 33\% \quad \frac{4}{12} \quad 1:3$$

(b) The following table lists some vulgar fractions. Complete the table to show equivalent values in different forms.

The shading is there to help you.

vulgar fraction	$\frac{1}{5}$	$\frac{1}{10}$	$\frac{1}{3}$	$\frac{2}{3}$	$\frac{1}{4}$	$\frac{1}{2}$	$\frac{1}{9}$	$\frac{1}{100}$	$\frac{1}{8}$	$\frac{1}{50}$
finite decimal fraction										
infinite recurring decimal fraction										
percentage										
ratio										

Vulgar fractions

B3

When vulgar fractions include large numbers like $\frac{23}{87}$ they can be difficult to visualize. One strategy for getting a feel for the difficult fraction is to compare it with easier fractions, and this can be done mentally. Without using a calculator or converting fractions to decimals, state which of the fractions below lie between $\frac{1}{4}$ and $\frac{2}{3}$. Describe your strategy for reaching a decision in each case.

> Think how the value of a fraction is altered by making the denominator bigger (or smaller).

$$\frac{1}{5} \qquad \frac{100}{399} \qquad \frac{3}{7} \qquad \frac{200}{301} \qquad \frac{3}{60}$$

Flexible use of fractions

B4

It is useful to be able to use different forms of fractions flexibly. This question focuses on the equivalence of vulgar fractions, decimals, percentages and ratio.

Complete this number grid by adding together two adjacent numbers in one row to calculate a number in the row above. For example a fifth and a tenth in the bottom row have been added to give three tenths and this has been written as the decimal fraction 0.3 in the row above.

ratio			260:100		
percentage	70%		150%			30%
decimal fraction		0.7			0.3	
vulgar fraction	$\frac{1}{10}$			$\frac{1}{5}$		$\frac{1}{10}$

> Treat this as a puzzle. Look for clues by asking 'What do I need to know to fill in this box?'

The four rules with vulgar fractions

Fluency

B5

You need to be well practised in using the four rules with vulgar fractions. This is an important set of skills in its own right but it also provides a background for further understanding. You can practise an appropriate level of fluency by completing the adjacent table.

a	$\frac{3}{5}$	$\frac{2}{5}$	$3\frac{1}{7}$	$3\frac{1}{7}$
b	$\frac{1}{5}$	$\frac{1}{7}$	$1\frac{4}{7}$	$1\frac{1}{5}$
$a + b$				
$a - b$				
$a \times b$				
$a \div b$				
$b \div a$				

> You may find it hard to recall what you were taught. Check the feedback. Refer to *Lessons: Fractions* in Book 2.

Relating vulgar fractions and decimal fractions

B6

You should be confident and agile moving between vulgar fractions and decimal fractions.

(a) Convert $\frac{3}{8}$ to a decimal fraction.

(b) Convert $\frac{1}{3}$ to a decimal fraction and use this result to express $\frac{2}{3}$ and $\frac{3}{3}$ as decimal fractions. Comment on your results.

(c) Convert 0.625 to a vulgar fraction.

(d) Convert 0.161616... to a vulgar fraction.

> Do not use a calculator.

> You probably need to check the feedback.

B7

Applications in geometry

Some of the most interesting applications of number can be found in geometry.

$\triangle ABC$ is an object which has been enlarged to become the image $\triangle A'B'C'$. Study the information in the diagram.

The technical terms *object* and *image* can be understood by studying the diagram.

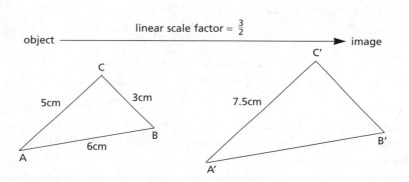

(a) Calculate the lengths of $A'B'$ and $B'C'$.

Linear scale factor

(b) What is the linear scale factor for the enlargement $\triangle A'B'C \rightarrow \triangle ABC$?

Linear scale factor refers to how much the lines have increased.

(c) The area of $\triangle ABC$ is 7.5cm². What is the area of $\triangle A'B'C'$?

Area scale factor

(d) What is the area scale factor for the enlargement $\triangle A'B'C' \rightarrow \triangle ABC$?

Scale factor refers to how much the area has increased.

Ratio and quotient

(e) Evaluate the ratio $A'B': AB$.

(f) Evaluate the ratio $AC: A'C'$.

(g) Evaluate the quotient (area of $\triangle A'B'C'$) ÷ (area of $\triangle ABC$).

Percentage

(h) Calculate the area of $\triangle ABC$ as a percentage of the area of $\triangle A'B'C'$.

(i) Study this diagram:

linear scale factor = $\frac{3}{2}$ linear scale factor = $\frac{2}{5}$

linear scale factor =   linear scale factor =

C'

C''

C

B''

5cm   3cm   B' A''

C   B A'

6cm   linear scale factor =

A

linear scale factor =

Calculate $\frac{3}{2} \times \frac{2}{5}$ and $\frac{5}{2} \times \frac{2}{3}$ and relate your calculations to the diagram above.

Linking different forms
for fractions

Percentage increase
and decrease

B8

Confidence with fractions and scale factors can transfer to confidence
with percentages once the links and connections between all three can
be seen.

(a) I extravagantly spent £84 in my favourite restaurant knowing that I
qualified for a 10% discount (for being a loyal customer). I was rather
alarmed to see that the new management had imposed a compulsory
15% service charge. The waiter was unsure whether to give me my
discount and then impose the service charge, or to impose the service
charge and then calculate the discount. Being sympathetic to my slight
annoyance at the service charge he allowed me to decide how to
calculate the bill. Which method would be to my advantage? Carefully
explain your view.

> Work carefully. Do not
> make any assumptions.

(b) After I had paid my bill the waiter started chatting amiably. He
showed me the £21 service charge that he had collected from an earlier
customer (on his first visit to the restaurant). What was the charge to
that customer?

B9

A question in a mental test asked for the original cost of an item that
had been reduced in a sale by 10% to £180. A child worked out in his
head that 10% of £180 was £18 and added the £18 to £180 to make £198.
Explain why this is wrong.

B10

Leading up to Christmas the price of a toy was increased by 10%.
In the January sales it was reduced by 10%. How did the sale price
compare with the original price before the Christmas increase?

> The answer is not
> obvious.

Scales on maps

B11

(a) I am planning a walking holiday. The scale of my map is
1 : 100 000. How far will I actually walk when I plan a journey that
measures 12.5cm on my map?

(b) Part of my holiday is covered by a map with scale 1 : 250 000.
One day I actually walk 38Km. What would that measure on
my map?

B12

You may have noticed when driving that you are sometimes
warned of the steepness of approaching hills by a road sign with
10% written on it. Although this is only an approximation, it could be
interpreted in two different ways. It might compare the vertical rise
with the horizontal distance. Alternatively it might compare the
vertical rise with the distance you travel on the road. Draw diagrams
for each of these interpretations and note which interpretation
indicates the steeper hill.

> Draw diagrams to make
> sense of the question.
> Then try to answer it.

Task C: Generalized arithmetic

Algebra as generalized arithmetic

Algebra is often perceived as difficult. One reason for this is that it is usually introduced as a subject separated from other areas of mathematics with rules and conventions that do not seem to relate to anything tangible. This task looks at algebra as generalized arithmetic. It is through algebra that arithmetic operations can be defined and properties of number studied. Algebra allows us to study just one generalized case rather than exhaustively examining every possible example. There are certain conventions that apply to arithmetical operations that are used internationally and it is this commonality across countries that makes mathematics such a powerful means of communication.

> You may like to read *Key ideas: Algebra* before doing this task.

C1

Conventions for arithmetic operations

It is important to know the conventions for arithmetical operations particularly when using a calculator.

> Look this up in *Feedback: Task C* if you have forgotten the conventions.

(a) Brackets are used to specify a particular order of operations. In the absence of brackets certain conventions apply. In the following calculation describe the correct order of operations and work out the answer.

$$7 + 6 \times 3$$

Using a calculator

(b) Some calculators are not programmed to follow these conventions but perform each operation as it is entered. What answer would such a calculator obtain?

Relating algebra to arithmetic

(c) The same conventions apply to algebra.

$$\text{If } b = 5 \text{ calculate } 4 + 5b$$

C2

Using brackets

Brackets can change the order of operations. Put brackets in the following calculations to obtain the correct answer.

(a) $2.2 - 3.3 + 4.4 - 5.5 + 6.6 = {}^-8.8$
(b) $2.2 - 3.3 + 4.4 - 5.5 + 6.6 = 4.4$
(c) $2.2 - 3.3 + 4.4 - 5.5 + 6.6 = 6.6$
(d) $2.2 - 3.3 + 4.4 - 5.5 + 6.6 = {}^-6.6$

C3

Identifying errors

Explain why the following calculations are incorrect and give the correct answer.

(a) $32 \div (8 \div 4) = 1$ (c) $14 - 3 \times 2 = 22$
(b) $36 \div (4 + 2) = 11$ (d) $25 - (6 - 9) = 10$

> The most common error made when using a calculator is to enter each operation in the order it is written.

C4

Entering complex calculations on a calculator

Work out the following calculation in your head and check the answer with a calculator.

$$120 \div \left[33 - \left(\frac{2 \times 6}{4} \right) \right]$$

> Start working from inside the inner bracket.

C5

Using algebra to express statements in arithmetic

Algebra can be used to express simple statements concisely and elegantly. Express the following statements algebraically.

(a) The sum of two numbers.

(b) The difference between two numbers.

(c) The product of two numbers.

(d) The quotient of two numbers.

(e) The square of a number.

(f) The square-root of a number.

(g) The sum of a number and its square.

> Each statement should be preceded by 'let the number(s) be ...'.

C6

Using algebra to express statements in geometry

Algebra can also be used to express geometric relationships. Express the following relationships algebraically.

(a) The area of a rectangle with sides of length x and y.

(b) The perimeter of a rectangle with sides of length a and b.

(c) The area of a square with sides of length c.

(d) The area of a triangle with base of length b and height h.

(e) The area of a trapezium with parallel sides of length a and b and perpendicular distance between them h.

> The algebraic expressions for these geometric relationships are called formulae.

C7

Using algebra for number puzzles

Algebra can be used to devise number puzzles to amaze your friends. Use algebra to show how to get the answer to the following problem.

A boy gave his friend a puzzle. 'Think of a number, double it, add nine, add the number you first thought of, divide the total by three and subtract three from the result. You should have the number you first thought of.'

> The algebraic statement is easier to follow than the words.

C8

Using algebra to express number operations

Numerical calculations can be written concisely in algebraic form and regular use of letters for numbers improves fluency. Complete the table below.

a	b	c	ab	ac	$a(b + c)$	$a(b - c)$
10	17	3				
5			15	30		
8					72	40
0.2			0.06		0.16	

Using algebra to practise number work

C9

Complete the following table.

a	b	a^2	$(a + b)^2$	$2a + b$	$2(a + b)$	$\frac{1}{a}$
5	3					
		64		10		
				17	20	
				22.5		0.1

> Remember the correct order of operations.

Interpreting mathematical statements

C10

There are sometimes different ways of interpreting spoken mathematics. For example, the statement 'three x squared minus nine' can be interpreted in the following three ways:

$$3x^2 - 9, \quad 3(x^2 - 9) \quad \text{and} \quad (3x)^2 - 9$$

A pupil was asked to complete a table with these three expressions heading the columns but her dog chewed her exercise book and she had to rewrite the table. Decide which order to enter the expressions in the table and complete all the missing entries.

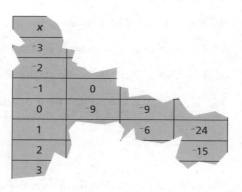

> Inspect the table and look for clues.

Using algebra to express number properties

C11

Properties of numbers can be expressed algebraically. Use what you know about certain types of numbers to express any number with the following names or properties algebraically.

(a) Any even number.

(b) Any odd number.

(c) Any number divisible by seven.

(d) Any square number.

(e) Any triangle number.

(f) Any cubic number.

> Consider what is special about each type of number.

Using algebra to express rules

C12

(a) Some rules for divisibility can be expressed algebraically. The rule for divisibility by nine is that the sum of the digits is divisible by nine. If you have a three digit number with digits a, b and c write down the rule for divisibility of nine for this number.

(b) Can you deduce from (a) a rule for divisibility by three?

C13

Algebraic factorization is often presented as something distinct from number. This question shows how number and algebra are closely linked.

(a) Write down all the factors of 18.

(b) Write down the prime factors of 20.

(c) Write down the common factors of 45 and 60.

(d) Write down the highest common factor of 42, 63 and 98.

(e) Write down factors of xyz.

(f) Write down a common factor of $2a$ and $2b$.

(g) Write down a common factor of $3ax$ and $5ay$.

(h) Write down a common factor of $(x-1)(x+2)$ and $(x-1)(x-3)$.

(i) Factorize $(x-1)(x+2)+(x-1)(x-3)$.

Relating factors in number to factors in algebra

> One factor of eighteen is six. Eighteen is divisible by six.

C14

You can use your knowledge of algebra to make number calculations easier.

(a) Given that $(a+b)^2 = a^2 + 2ab + b^2$ complete the following:
$$31^2 = (30+1)^2 =$$

(b) Use the same method as in (a) to work out 53^2.

(c) Given that $(a-b)(a+b) = a^2 - b^2$ complete the following:
$$49 \times 51 = (50-1)(50+1) =$$

(d) Use the same method as in (c) to work out 28×32.

Using algebra to make number calculations easier

> The most common error is to omit the term $2ab$.

> The expression $a^2 - b^2$ is called the difference of two squares.

C15

True or false? Say if the phrases below are true or false for all numbers. If they are true for some numbers specify what these numbers may be. Justify your answers.

(a) It doesn't matter which way round you multiply two numbers.

(b) It doesn't matter which way round you divide two numbers.

(c) The sum of two numbers is equal to their product.

(d) The square of the product of two numbers is equal to the product of their squares.

(e) The sum of the squares of two numbers is equal to the square of their sum.

Using algebra to justify answers

> You may like to read *Key ideas: Proof*.

C16

A mathematical investigation asks what shapes have the same numerical value for their area as for their perimeter.

(a) How would you express this algebraically for any rectangle?

(b) Are there any squares for which the statement is true?

Using algebra in investigations

Task D: Pattern and proof

Rules, patterns and relationships

When we do problems, investigations or experiments we sometimes get results that obey rules, patterns or relationships that we want to generalize. Algebra offers us the means to communicate these results concisely and precisely. The letter n is usually used to denote the general term in a sequence of numbers. The letters x and y are normally used to denote variables, particularly when we represent results graphically using Cartesian co-ordinates.

See *Key ideas: Proof.*

D1

Sequence of odd numbers

1, 3, 5, 7 ... is the sequence of 'odd' numbers. (Four numbers in a sequence are insufficient for generalization – you can only guess. However, in this question you are told specifically that the sequence is of odd numbers and this is sufficient for generalization.)

It is easy to jump to conclusions when you spot a pattern with numbers. Always check that you have sufficient information.

(a) Write down the next four odd numbers.

(b) Explain how you worked them out.

(c) Write down the tenth odd number.

The nth odd number

(d) Write down the nth odd number.

Difference between terms

(e) What is the difference between successive terms of the sequence of odd numbers?

The sum of n odd numbers

(f) What is the sum of the first n odd numbers?

D2

Sequence of triangle numbers

1, 3, 6, 10 ... This is the sequence of 'triangle' numbers. (Again you are given additional information sufficient to define the sequence.)

(a) Explain why they are called triangle numbers.

(b) Write down the next four numbers of the sequence.

(c) Explain how you worked them out.

(d) Work out the tenth triangle number.

The nth triangle number

(e) Write down the nth triangle number.

Difference between terms

(f) What can you say about the differences between successive terms of the sequence?

The difference between each term can give you clues about the sequence.

Relating one sequence to another

(g) How does the sequence 3, 5, 8, 12, ... relate to the sequence of triangle numbers?

(h) Use this relationship to write down a possible nth term of this sequence in its simplest form. (Why can't you be definite about this generalization?)

D3

The general term of a sequence

Algebraic expressions: linear

The general term of a sequence of numbers is given by $3n - 2$.

(a) Write down the first five numbers of this sequence.

Start with $n = 1$

(b) The algebraic expression $3n - 2$ is linear. What does this mean?

Difference between terms

(c) What is the difference between each term of the sequence?

D4

The general term of a sequence is given by $n^2 + 1$.

(a) Write down the first five terms of this sequence. Start with $n = 1$.

Algebraic expressions: quadratic

(b) The algebraic expression $n^2 + 1$ is quadratic. What does this mean?

Difference between terms

(c) Work out the difference between successive terms and then the difference between successive differences (called the second differences). What do you notice?

Algebraic expressions: cubic

(d) If the general term of a sequence were cubic, make a conjecture about the third differences.

> If the first differences do not give you the clues try the second differences and so on.

D5

Making assumptions

(a) A child doing an investigation produced the results 2, 4, 8, 16, and assumed that the next number would be 32. What assumption has she made and what would be the nth term of such a sequence?

Using algorithms

(b) A second child continued the investigation and found that in fact the next two numbers in the sequence were 31 and 57. Inspect the successive differences and suggest what the next two numbers might be. What can you say about the general term of such a sequence?

> You still do not have sufficient information to be absolutely certain about this sequence.

Getting information from an equation

(c) The nth term of a sequence is given by $5n - 7$. What information can you get from the equation $5n - 7 = 148$?

The Fibonacci sequence

(d) 1, 1, 2, 3, 5, 8, 13 ... This sequence of numbers is called the Fibonacci sequence. Work out the next five numbers in the sequence and explain how you worked them out.

D6

Pascal's triangle

```
              1
           1     1
        1     2     1
     1     3     3     1
  1     4     6     4     1
1     5    10    10     5     1
```

> Pascal was one of the first mathematicians to do proof by induction, in 1653.

This array of numbers is called Pascal's triangle.

(a) Describe how each row is calculated from the one above.

(b) Write down the next three rows in the array.

The sum of each row

(c) Work out the sum of each row. What will be the sum of the nth row?

Coefficients

(d) Work out $(a + b)^2$ and inspect the coefficients of each term. Which row of Pascal's triangle represents these coefficients?

D7

The sum of the counting numbers

There is a neat way of finding the sum of the counting numbers 1, 2, 3 ... Write down the numbers one to ten and directly underneath write them down in reverse order.

> See *Key ideas: Proof*.

(a) What do you notice about the sum of each column?

(b) Use this to write down the sum of the first ten counting numbers.

(c) Use your result to write down the sum of the first n counting numbers.

Squares on a chessboard

Starting with small boards

Generalizing

Using a formula

Geometric patterns

Using the geometrical structure

Generalizations as formulae

Applications in medicine

D8

Children were asked to investigate how many squares were on a chessboard. They broke down the task and started with smaller boards. They found the following pattern:

1×1 board   1 square
2×2 board   1 big square and 4 little squares
3×3 board   1 big square, 4 smaller squares and 9 little squares

(a) Continue the pattern and work out the total number of squares for an 8×8 board (the chess board).

(b) How would you work out the total number of squares on an $n \times n$ board?

(c) Check that the formula $\frac{n}{6}(n+1)(2n+1)$ gives the total number of squares for any board.

> One way to solve a problem systematically is to break it down into more manageable tasks.

> Although this investigation is often done by young children the formula for the number of squares is complex.

D9

Generalizations may result from geometric patterns.

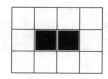

Black tiles are completely surrounded by white tiles exactly as shown in the diagram.

(a) How many white tiles are required to surround a row of 15 black tiles?

(b) How many white tiles are required to surround a row of n black tiles?

(c) The pattern is changed so that there are now two rows of black tiles. How many white tiles are required to surround n columns of black tiles?

(d) The pattern is changed so that there are m rows of black tiles. How many white tiles are required to surround n columns of black tiles?

(e) Justify your answer to (d) by referring to the geometrical structure of the pattern.

> You do not need to waste time drawing out different examples because the answer lies in the geometric structure.

D10

(a) Generalizations can be used as formulae.

Rectangles are drawn so that the length is always two units more than the width. Write down formulae for the area and perimeter of these rectangles.

(b) Formulae may be used in many walks of life.

Doses of a particular medicine are given in direct proportion to the weight of the patient. If one patient who weighs 65Kg is given 5ml of medicine, what is the dose (to the nearest millilitre) for someone who weighs 80Kg?

(c) Write down a formula to calculate the doses of medicine in (b).

> It is important to use the correct formula, particularly in the field of medicine.

D11

You are often offered special deals but you need to check them to see whether you are really going to gain.

A customer is offered a special tariff for a mobile phone. Monthly bills are calculated by adding the standard charge of £25 to the cost of the calls. Calls are charged at x pence per second and 15 minutes of calls are free.

(a) Work out the monthly bill when the customer used the phone for 2 hours 35 mins 10 secs and $x = 1$.

(b) Write down a formula for calculating the monthly bills.

(c) The customer could have taken a different tariff with the same standard charge but instead of having any free calls all the calls cost half the price. Which is the better deal?

> It is not immediately obvious which is the best deal.

D12

You can use algebra to provide a convincing argument or proof.

(a) Give precise details of the numbers for which the following statement is true:

'The sum of four even numbers is divisible by four.'

> You can read more about this in *Key ideas: Proof*.

(b)

Sun	Mon	Tue	Wed	Thu	Fri	Sat
		1	2	3	4	5
6	7	8	9	10	11	12
13	14	15	16	17	18	19
20	21	22	23	24	25	26
27	28	29	30	31		

On a calendar take a block of four numbers and add them up. Explain your results and make a conjecture. Use algebra to explain why your conjecture must always be true.

> It is the structure of the calendar that gives you the clues.

(c) You may think that you have made a discovery but can you be sure? If you cannot use algebra to prove it you may have to keep trying until you find a counter example to disprove your theory. You may be able to spot a counter example right away from the algebraic structure.

Work out the value of $n^2 - n + 11$ for $n = 1, 2, 3, 4 \ldots$
What sort of numbers have been produced? Is there a counter-example to your conjecture?

D13

When you know a given property you can use it to deduce other properties.

Given that the sum of the interior angles of a triangle is 180° deduce the sum of the interior angles of:

(a) a quadrilateral

(b) a pentagon

(c) an n-sided polygon.

> There is a certain elegance in developing an argument that starts with 'given that ... then it follows that ...'.

Task E: Equations and graphs

Doing basic arithmetic implies the use of algebra.

Using graphs to represent solutions

Using symbolic notation

Whenever you work out even simple things such as how many fours make twenty-four you are implicitly forming and solving an equation. You could write it more formally as $4x = 24$ and in your head you could probably work out $24 ÷ 4$ to get your answer. When the problem is more complex you need to know how to set out the equation formally using symbols and you need to know the rules and conventions that are used to solve it. The answer may not be straightforward and you may need to draw a graph to show all the possible solutions to your problem.

See *Key ideas: Algebra* for a discussion of thinking algebraically.

E1

Use symbols to help you write the following problems as equations and then solve them. (Solving an equation may give you one answer or a set of answers.)

(a) How many sevens in 1484?

(b) Think of a number, double it and add 3. If the answer is 15 what was the number?

(c) A child saved £1.30 of her pocket money and used the rest to buy five packets of crisps. If she had a total of £3 pocket money how much did each packet of crisps cost?

Work in pence.

(d) A number squared is 40. What is the number?

Use a calculator.

(e) When you add 5 to a number you get the same answer as when you subtract 3 from double the number. What is the number?

(f) A quarter of a number is 0.5. What is the number?

(g) Thirty-six divided by a number is eight. What is the number?

(h) The sum of two numbers is ten.

See *Key ideas: Algebra* for a discussion of presenting anwers.

(i) The difference between two numbers is two.

Linear equations

A graphical representation

E2

(a) The three sets of equations in the table below are all 'linear equations'. Explain why they are called linear and describe how you can tell by looking at an equation that it is linear.

(b) Draw three pairs of axes with $^-8 \leq x \leq 8$ and $^-8 \leq y \leq 8$. Inspect the following three sets of equations. Represent the solutions for each set by drawing graphs for each set on a different pair of axes.

Set A	Set B	Set C
$y = x$	$y = 2x$	$y = 3x$
$y = x + 4$	$y = 3x$	$y = 3x + 4$
$y = x - 4$	$y = {}^-4x$	$y = 3x - 4$

$y = mx + c$

(c) Inspect the equation $y = mx + c$. Use it to describe the appearance in graph form of the different equations in the table above.

A linear equation

E3

Inspect the equation $F = \frac{9}{5}C + 32$ and its corresponding graph drawn below.

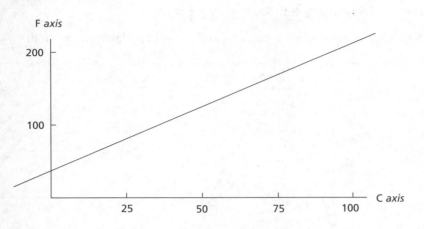

Just think of the graph as representing the relationship (nothing to do with temperature).

(a) Discuss the appearance of the graph in relation to $y = mx + c$.

(b) Use the graph to estimate the omitted values in the table.

C	0	100			35
F			98.4	80	

Fahrenheit-Celsius conversion graph

(c) Interpret C and F as the number of degrees Celsius and Fahrenheit respectively. The equation $F = \frac{9}{5}C + 32$ expresses the relationship between these scales of temperature. Make a note near each pair of equivalent temperatures of how hot each is (use everyday examples).

This is now giving it a real-life interpretation.

(d) Write down how you would explain to a friend on the phone how to convert a temperature in degrees Celsius to degrees Fahrenheit and how to convert a temperature in degrees Fahrenheit to degrees Celsius.

(e) Inspect this Fahrenheit/Celsius conversion graph.

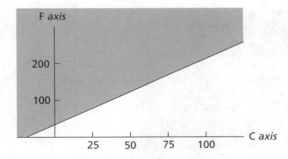

Interpreting an inequality

The shaded region represents all the points where $F > \frac{9}{5}C + 32$. Describe what this region represents in terms of Celsius and Fahrenheit degrees.

Think of the shaded area as an infinite number of points.

Simultaneous equations

E4

(a) In E1 (h) and (i) you were asked for the equations $x + y = 10$ and $x - y = 2$. Draw the graphs of these equations on the same pair of axes.

(b) Use the graph to find which number pair satisfies both equations (that is, solve them simultaneously).

(c) You are given the information that the sum of two numbers is 7 and their product is 12. Write these two statements as algebraic equations. Look at the two equations and find the solution by inspection. Draw a graph to illustrate your result.

(d) Solve the simultaneous equations in (c) using an algebraic method.

E5

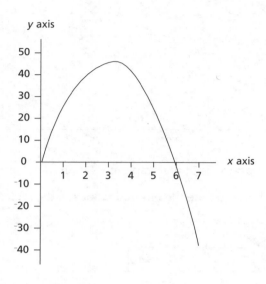

Graph of a quadratic equation

(a) The graph shows the solutions of the equation $y = 45 - 5(x-3)^2$. Complete the table and check that the results are confirmed by the graph.

x	0	1	2	3	4	5	6	7
y	0	25				25	0	‾35

A distance-time graph

Reading graphs

(b) Interpret the graph as relating the height of a stone in metres (y) and the time during which it was in flight (x).
Complete this table:

maximum height achieved	
time to reach maximum height	
duration of flight	
height after 2 seconds	
height after 6 seconds	

Interpretation

(c) Create some interpretation of the height indicated by the graph and the table of values after 6 seconds.

(d) Calculate a value for the height (y) after the stone has been in flight for ‾1 seconds. Discuss how this can be interpreted.

E6

Graph of a quadratic equation

(a) The graph shows the solutions of the equation $y = 5(x-3)^2 + 45$. Study the table and check that the results are confirmed by the graph.

x	0	1	2	3	4	5	6
y	90	65	50	45	50	65	90

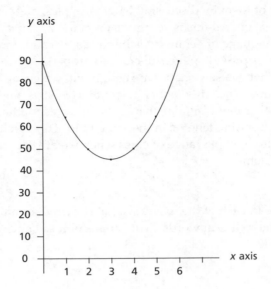

Interpreting a distance-time graph

(b) Interpret the graph as relating height in metres (y) and the time (x).
Create some interpretation of what this graph could represent.

E7

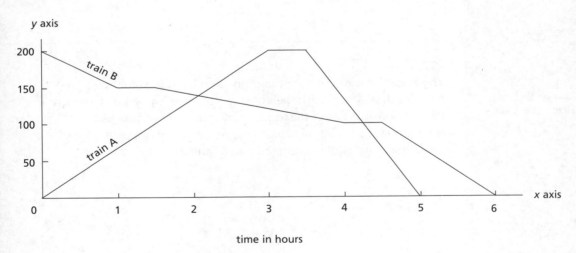

A story behind the graph

Interpret this graph as representing the journeys of two trains (A and B)
travelling between London and Bristol (a distance of 200Km).
y represents the distance from London (in Km) and x represents the
time of travel (in hours).

(a) Describe the journey of train A.
(b) Describe the journey of train B.
(c) Write down when the trains passed each other.

Task F: Geometry

When we do maths we deal with two- and three-dimensional shapes and make sense of them by discussing lengths, angles, areas, volumes, parallelism and so on. All this is summarized in the key idea of geometry. The language of geometry is important because individual words and phrases provide powerful clues to properties and relationships. When we say 'shapes are congruent' we get an immediate picture of the edges equal in length as well as angles equal in size. On the other hand 'similar shapes' have corresponding angles equal and corresponding lengths in the same ratio. This careful use of language provides a whole range of clues when we are dealing with geometrical problems.

Words and phrases provide powerful clues

See *Key ideas: The language of maths.*

F1

Inspect the angle in each of the diagrams. Label each diagram by selecting from the technical words: acute angle; obtuse angle; right angle; reflex angle.

Technical words for angles

An angle is a measure of turn. These technical words give a sense of the size of the angle.

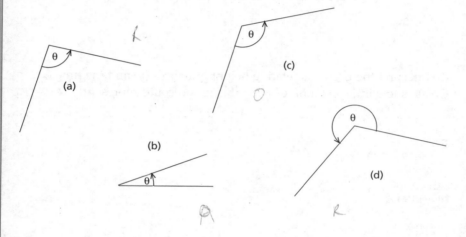

F2

The angles marked in each diagram are related in some way. Label each diagram with the appropriate technical words to describe the relationship. Select the appropriate words from this list: corresponding angles; alternate angles; vertically opposite angles; supplementary angles; complementary angles.

Technical words to describe relationships

Inspect the words and note the logic in the language.

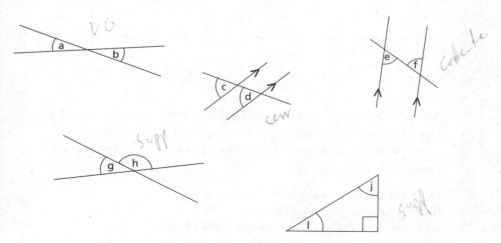

Looking for clues

F3

Inspect this diagram.
AB is parallel to CD.

Refer to the feedback if you do not understand the way the angles have been labelled.

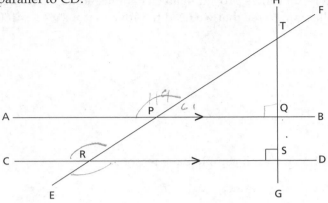

Relationships between pairs of angles

(a) Complete this table to show the relationship between pairs of angles.

There may be more than one angle or no angle at all with the specified relationship.

Angle	$\widehat{APT}$	$\widehat{PRS}$	$\widehat{HTF}$
corresponding	$\widehat{CRP}$		
alternate	APR		
vertically opposite			
supplementary			
complementary			

(b) Given that angle APT = 119° calculate angles PTQ and ERS.

Similar triangles

(c) Identify two triangles in the diagram that are similar, giving reasons.

(d) Let the ratio of the lengths of the lines SQ : QT = 1 : 3.

Calculate the ratio of the lengths of the lines RP : PT.
Calculate the ratio of the lengths of the lines SQ : ST.

(e) If the length of the line ST = 20cm calculate the length of SQ.

....

F4

Construction using a ruler and a pair of compasses

Using a ruler and a pair of compasses only construct the following:

(a) The perpendicular bisector of a line AB.

These constructions relate to the properties of circles.

(b) The bisector of angle ABC.

(c) An equilateral triangle ABC with edges 5cm.

(d) Construct triangle ABC such that AB = 7cm, BC = 5.5cm and AC = 6.2cm.

(e) If one edge AB of a triangle ABC is 10cm, what can you say about the lengths of edges AC and BC for the triangle to be possible?

The sum of the interior angles of a triangle

Studying a proof

Giving reasons

F5

The sum of the interior angles of a triangle is 180°. This important geometrical result can be proved in an elegant fashion. Inspect the following diagram to see that we need to prove that $x + y + z = 180$.

This result is used as the basis for other geometric proofs.

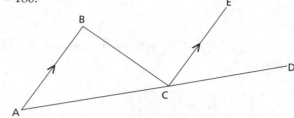

Now study the proof and complete the reasons.

To prove that $x + y + z = 180$:

Construction:
produce AC to D;
draw CE parallel
to AB.

The construction of a parallel line makes this proof possible.

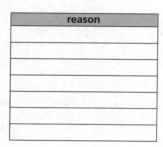

Proof:
x = angle BAC = angle ECD
y = angle ABC = angle BCE
z = angle ACB
$x + y + z$ = BAC + ABC + ACB
        = ECD + BCE + ACB
But ECD + BCE + ACB = 180
$\therefore x + y + z = 180$

reason

F6

Angle in a semi-circle

Any angle in a semi-circle is a right angle. Study the proof for this and complete by providing the reasons.

To prove that angle ABC = 90°:

Giving reasons

In the circle O is
the centre and
AC is a diameter.

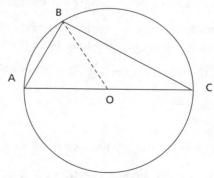

Remember that the radius of a circle is constant.

Proof:
OA = OB = OC
angle OBA = angle OAB = x
angle OBC = angle OCB = y
angle ABC = $x + y$
angle OAB + angle ABC + angle BCA = 180
$x + (x + y) + y = 180$
$2x + 2y = 180$
$\therefore x + y = 90$

reason

F7

(a) Sketch the locus of a point that moves in a plane such that its distance from a fixed point is constant.

(b) Sketch the locus of a point that moves in a plane such that its distance from two fixed points is constant.

(c) A rectangular garden measuring 10m by 5m has a tree at one corner and another at the centre. A lawn is laid so that it is always 0.5m from the surrounding fence and 1.5m from each tree. Sketch a plan for the garden shading the region where the grass is laid.

> A locus is a set of points generated by a point or line moving according to a rule.

The locus of a point

F8

(a) The letter F is rotated from position A to position B. Using a ruler and a pair of compasses find the centre of rotation and, using a protractor, measure the angle of rotation.

> The construction is described in detail in the feedback.

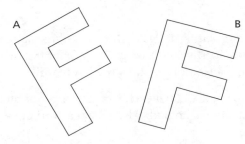

Finding the centre of rotation

(b) Using a ruler and a pair of compasses reflect triangle ABC in the mirror line m.

> Do not guess at the line perpendicular to the mirror line but construct it using compasses and ruler.

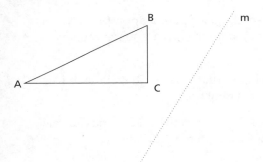

Reflecting in a mirror line

F9

Draw a pair of axes such that $^-6 \leq x \leq 6$ and $^-6 \leq y \leq 6$.

Draw triangle ABC with co-ordinates (1, 1), (3, 5) and (4, 2) respectively. Carry out the following transformations and describe the effect of each transformation on the co-ordinates. Also state which transformations result in a triangle congruent to triangle ABC.

(a) Reflect triangle ABC in the x-axis.

(b) Reflect triangle ABC in the y-axis.

(c) Reflect triangle ABC in the line $y = x$.

(d) Rotate triangle ABC 90° clockwise, centre the origin.

(e) Rotate triangle ABC 180°, centre the origin.

(f) Enlarge triangle ABC, centre the origin, linear scale factor 0.5.

> See B7 in *Audit: Task B.*

Transformations on Cartesian co-ordinates

Task G: Properties of shapes

Using correct names and terminology

It is in geometry that we so often find the most exciting and challenging problems. Fluency in number and a sound knowledge of algebra both help in solving such problems. It is important to use the correct names and terminology when talking and writing about shapes and their properties. It is all too easy to assume that a shape is regular or that its base is horizontal.

G1

(a)

You can draw eight *different* triangles on three-by-three square lattices by joining three dots as vertices. A triangle is *different* if it is not a reflection, rotation or translation of one already identified.

Naming triangles

Draw each different triangle. Label each triangle appropriately: right-angled; acute-angled; obtuse angled. Also label each triangle: scalene, isosceles, equilateral.

Naming quadrilaterals

(b) Using the same three-by-three grid and joining just four dots at a time you can draw twelve different convex quadrilaterals.

Draw each quadrilateral. Label each quadrilateral appropriately: irregular quadrilateral; trapezium; parallelogram; square; rhombus; rectangle; kite.

Drawing lines of symmetry

(c) For each of the triangles and quadrilaterals you have drawn use dotted lines to show any lines of symmetry.

Working out area

(d) The distance between each of the dots on the grid is one centimetre. Work out the area of each triangle and each quadrilateral.

G2

Properties of quadrilaterals

(a) Describe each of the following shapes:

quadrilateral; parallelogram; rhombus; rectangle; square; trapezium.

True or false?

(b) Use your descriptions above to deduce whether the following statements are true or false, giving reasons for your answers.

'All squares are rectangles.'
'Squares, rectangles and rhombi are all parallelograms.'
'All trapezia are rectangles.'
'All parallelograms have two lines of symmetry.'

Tessellations

(c) Any quadrilateral can be used to draw a tessellation (a tiling pattern without any gaps). Draw a diagram to illustrate such a tessellation and explain why you can tessellate any quadrilateral.

(d) Which *regular* polygons can be used to draw a tessellation? Give reasons for your answer.

See *Key ideas: The language of maths.*

A good way to do this is to use a pin board and elastic bands.

See the *Glossary* if you have forgotten the terms.

You can work out all the areas by inspecting the shapes for right-angled triangles.

In this case a tessellation is made using one shape. You can draw tessellations with two shapes, e.g. with an octagon and a square.

Circumference and diameter

G3

(a) In a practical lesson in which some children were measuring the circumference and diameter of tins to the nearest millimetre they produced the following results.

	Tin						
	A	B	C	D	E	F	G
diameter (d) cm	8.5	7.2	10.7	9.3	6.5	5.5	4.2
circumference (C) cm	26.3	19.8	33.5	32.3	20.6	14.5	12.2

The nature of measurement means that these can only be approximate.

Checking results

Check which of these results are likely to be reasonable and explain why.

Sketching a net

(b) You want to make a label for a tin that will surround it exactly but not overlap. The diameter of the tin is 9cm and its height is 12cm. Sketch the label indicating its measurements.

First decide which approximation you will use for π.

Graphs to represent relationships

(c) The relationship between the circumference and diameter of circles can be represented by the following graph.

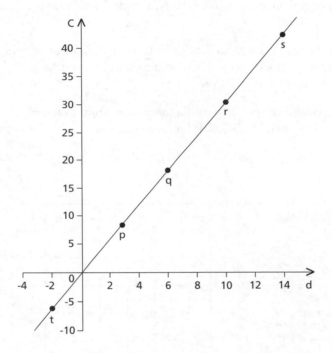

Working from the graph

Describe the circles represented by the points p, q, r, s and t and suggest possible cylindrical shapes for which these are the cross-sections.

It can be fun to imagine what shapes could be represented by points on the graph.

....

G4

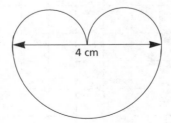

4 cm

Perimeter and area

Calculate the perimeter and area of this figure. (Use π = 3.14)

G5

In maths you sometimes work like a detective. In the following descriptions look for clues to identify the shapes and complete the grid below by ticking the relevant properties (some shapes will have several ticks).

Working like a detective

Looking for clues

Read *Key ideas: The nature of maths.*

Properties of diagonals

(a) This shape is a polygon. It has four sides equal in length. Its diagonals are equal and intersect at right angles.

Properties of angles

(b) This is a closed, flat shape. It has four angles. Its opposite angles are equal. Its diagonals are not equal and do not cross at right angles.

We often neglect to look at the diagonals of a shape but they can give us crucial information about its properties.

Capacity

(c) This shape has a capacity of one litre. It has a cross-section that is the same all the way through. The cross-section is hexagonal in shape.

Number of faces

(d) This shape has a volume of 24cm³. It has six faces. Each face has four interior angles of 90° and opposite edges equal.

The shape of faces

(e) The volume of this shape is a third of the volume of a cuboid. It has five faces. One face is a square and four faces are isosceles triangles.

Symmetry

(f) This shape has an angle sum of 540°. It has five lines of symmetry and rotational symmetry of order five. It cannot be used on its own to draw a tessellation.

Properties of diagonals

(g) This is a closed shape. Its two diagonals are equal in length but do not cross at right angles. It has zero volume.

(h) This shape is a polygon. Its two diagonals are not equal but cross at right angles.

Shape	a	b	c	d	e	f	g	h
2-D								
3-D								
regular								
quadrilateral								
parallelogram								
rectangle								
square								
rhombus								
pentagon								
cuboid								
cube								
prism								
pyramid								

G6

(a)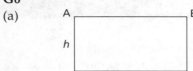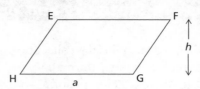

The formula for the area of the rectangle ABCD is *ah*. Explain why the formula for the area of the parallelogram EFGH is also *ah*.

(b)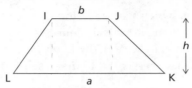

Use the formulae for the area of triangles and parallelograms to show that the formula for the area of a trapezium IJKL is $\frac{1}{2}(a+b)h$.

When you look at the parallelogram or trapezium imagine dotted lines drawn to help you.

G7

(a)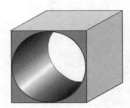

A cylindrical plug is cut from a cube of wood with edges 5cm. What volume of wood is wasted? (Use $\pi = 3.14$)

(b) Work out the percentage of wood wasted.

Look in the *Glossary* if you have forgotten the formulae.

G8

(a)

You want to design a container with a capacity of 1000cm³. You decide to make a prism with a hexagonal cross section of edge 6cm. What will be the height of the prism?

(b) The prism is made out of a sheet of plastic except for the lid. What area of plastic will be required to make the container?

Pythagoras' theorem for right-angled triangles: the square on the hypotenuse is equal to the sum of the squares on the other two sides.

G9

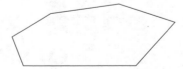

You use 100 centimetres of string to make polygons. You want to make the polygon with the greatest area. Make a conjecture about which polygon will give you the greatest area and draw a graph to illustrate your results.

Sidebar labels:

Area of a parallelogram

Area of a trapezium

Volume of a cube

Volume of a cylinder

Percentage

Working backwards

Maximum area with given perimeter

Task H: Statistics and probability

Statistics is ...

Probability is ...

Inspecting data

Comparing data

Different forms of representation

Statistics deals with the collection and presentation of data and its interpretation into information. In order to do this you must be able to use frequency tables, pictorial and graphical representation and measures such as median, mode, mean and range. The first part of this task indicates what it means to be able to use these statistical devices.

Another set of ideas which we use to interpret certain types of data is *probability*. Probability includes techniques we can use to answer questions that often begin with 'How likely is it ...?' The second part of this task outlines what is essential to make sense of probability.

This is discussed in more detail in *Feedback: Task H.*

H1

(a) Inspect each of the following sets of data and complete the table.

Data set A: 1, 1, 2, 2, 3, 3, 3, 4, 5, 6, 7
Data set B: 1, 1, 2, 2, 3, 3, 3, 4, 5, 6, 7, 1, 1, 2, 2, 3, 3, 3, 4, 5, 6, 7
Data set C: 2, 2, 4, 4, 6, 6, 6, 6, 8, 10, 12, 14

(b) Inspect the table and compare data sets A and B.

(c) Inspect the table and compare sets A and C.

	Data set A	Data set B	Data set C
sample size	11	22	11
smallest	1	1	2
largest	7	7	14
mean	3 36	3·36	6·7
median	3	3	6
mode	3	3	6
upper quartile	5	3·3	10
lower quartile	1·8	3·3	3·6
range	6	6	12

You have to be careful not to read more into these summary statistics than the figures tell you.

H2

Inspect the data from the two different surveys presented below.

Data can be presented in different forms. Which of these best conveys the information?

Survey 1: Survey of preferred form of travel

Form of travel	Number of people
bus	1200
train	400
walk	300
car	200
bicycle	300

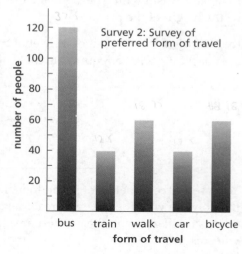

Survey 2: Survey of preferred form of travel

Interpreting data

(a) How many people took part in each survey?

(b) What is the most popular form of travel in each survey?

(c) What percentage of the total sample prefer each form of travel in each survey?

Pie chart

Interpreting data

H3
Inspect this pie chart as a representation of a set of data.

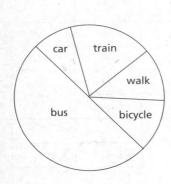

(a) How many people took part in the survey?

(b) What is the most popular form of travel?

(c) What percentage of the total sample prefer each form of travel?

(d) The title is missing from this diagram and so are the figures. Does this set of data relate to either of the surveys in H2?

> This is another way of representing information. Compare it with the previous two forms.

H4
Tadwell Sports Club held an election for President. There was some interest not only in who won but also in the way in which women voted. Study the following sets of data.

Votes for president at the AGM of Tadwell Sports Club 19.45 on Wednesday 2 May			

Candidate	Total number of votes	Candidate	Total number of women's votes
A	120	A	0
B	40	B	40
C	30	C	12
D	20	D	3
E	30	E	5

Descriptive statistics

(a) Simply by comparing the figures in the tables (without doing any calculations), what information can you extract from this data?

> Take care not to make inferences that do not come from the data itself.

Now do calculations to provide the following information.

Summary statistics

(b) How many people voted altogether?

(c) What percentage of the vote was won by the winning candidate?

(d) What percentage of the voting members at this meeting were women?

(e) What percentage of the women's vote did each candidate win?

(f) Which of these two sets of data could be summarized by the pie chart in H3?

Frequency tables

H5

Inspect the following sets of data.

Read *Feedback: Task H* to help you understand the entries in the table.

Survey of shoe sizes of 100 people interviewed in Accrington		
x	f	xf
5	3	15
6	6	36
7	15	105
8	20	160
9	28	252
10	22	220
11	5	55
12	1	12
	$\sum f = 100$	$\sum xf = 855$

Survey of shoe sizes of 100 people interviewed in Burnley		
x	f	xf
5	8	
6	9	
7	16	
8	18	
9	24	
10	19	
11	3	
12	3	
	$\sum f =$	$\sum xf =$

Completing frequency tables

(a) Inspect the first frequency table to see how it has been completed and complete the second frequency table in the same way.

Mean, mode and median

(b) Calculate the mean, mode and median for each set of data.

Mean, mode and median are all averages.

(c) Summarize in words the comparison between the two samples.

....

H6

Cumulative frequency table

Data on shoe sizes are collected from 400 people in Chelmsford. Inspect the cumulative frequency table and the cumulative frequency curve.

The first entry under *f* indicates that 18 people wear shoes less than or equal to size 5.

(a) Convince yourself that the cumulative frequency graph summarizes the data in the table (write a sentence that contains the main points).

Estimating the median

(b) Using the cumulative frequency curve calculate an estimate of the median and the upper and lower quartiles.

Cumulative frequency table: survey of shoe sizes of 400 people in Chelmsford			
x	f	x	f
≤ 5	18	≤ 9	294
≤ 6	47	≤ 10	367
≤ 7	109	≤ 11	390
≤ 8	195	≤ 12	400

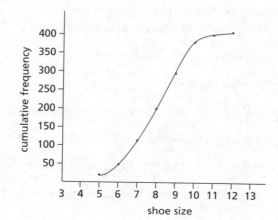

Probability

H7

In the following questions P (an event) stands for the probability of that event.

(a) A fair die is rolled. What is P(4)? $\frac{1}{4}$

(b) A coin is spun. What is P(H)? $\frac{1}{2}$

(c) A die is rolled and then a coin is spun. What is P(4, H)? $\frac{1}{4} \times \frac{1}{2} = \frac{1}{8}$

(d) Two fair dice are rolled. What is the probability of getting a total score of 4? $\frac{3}{36} - \frac{1}{12}$

(e) The probability of it raining today is $\frac{4}{10}$. The probability that I will take my umbrella is $\frac{2}{5}$. What is the probability that I will stay dry? $\frac{6}{10} \times \frac{2}{10}$ $\frac{12}{100}$

(f) Inspect the following statements.

'The probability of scoring 4 when I roll a die is $\frac{1}{6}$' is accurate and is based on the fact that the possibility space consists of six equally likely outcomes.

Equally likely outcomes

'The probability that it will rain today is $\frac{2}{3}$' is an estimate based on empirical data.

Estimated probability

Discuss these statements sufficiently to show that you understand the two different ways of calculating probabilities.

Studying an argument

(g) I feel convinced that there is a good chance that there is life on Mars. I argue that because there are two possibilities: (either there is life on Mars or there is not life on Mars) the probability that I am right is $\frac{1}{2}$. Does my calculation support my conviction?

> When outcomes are equally likely the probability can be calculated theoretically. Otherwise probability has to be calculated from experimental evidence.

H8

A tree diagram

Inspect this tree diagram for a two-stage experiment that involves drawing a card from a pack and then, without replacing it, drawing a second card. The letter C represents the event of drawing a court card. The letter L represents the event of drawing a number less than eleven. (An ace is not a court card; it is a number less than eleven.)

> The clue here is that cards are not replaced.

(a) Interpret each figure on the diagram.

(b) Use the diagram to calculate the probability of obtaining a court card and a number less than eleven.

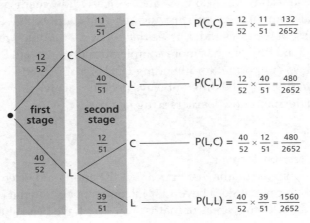

first stage / second stage

$$\frac{11}{51} \quad C \qquad P(C,C) = \frac{12}{52} \times \frac{11}{51} = \frac{132}{2652}$$

$$\frac{12}{52} \quad C$$

$$\frac{40}{51} \quad L \qquad P(C,L) = \frac{12}{52} \times \frac{40}{51} = \frac{480}{2652}$$

$$\frac{12}{51} \quad C \qquad P(L,C) = \frac{40}{52} \times \frac{12}{51} = \frac{480}{2652}$$

$$\frac{40}{52} \quad L$$

$$\frac{39}{51} \quad L \qquad P(L,L) = \frac{40}{52} \times \frac{39}{51} = \frac{1560}{2652}$$

Feedback

What is meant by feedback?

The feedback in this section contains answers, but not only answers. Where appropriate you are given specific help to get the right answer. More importantly, the feedback often discusses issues around the specific problem you are dealing with. It links the maths needed for one problem with ideas elsewhere in this book.

Learning new topics in maths sometimes seems difficult; it can be hard to get a 'feel' for the coherence of the subject. The feedback helps you make links. Links are at their most satisfying when they are made under the umbrella of a few relatively powerful ideas. For this reason you are often referred to the *Key ideas* section, and you should bear the key ideas in mind the whole time.

When you look at some of the tasks, you may find that you can cope with them without too much difficulty. Nevertheless, you should still read the feedback; it may suggest a way of thinking about a task which had not occurred to you. If you were studying to get a qualification in maths, this might not be quite so important – but you're not. Your needs as a learner of maths are related to your intention to teach. You have a special responsibility for the nature and quality of your learning. The purpose of the feedback is to provide an outline of what it means to think about maths in ways which are appropriate to teaching.

You may find when you look at the feedback (maybe for the answer, perhaps for the advice as well) that you will say 'If I had known that that was what was wanted, I could have done it'. But it is important to follow up the connecting ideas so you can see clearly how maths is coherent. It is also important to discuss the questions with others. Through discussion we can suddenly see that what we thought was straightforward and obvious has more complexities than we had appreciated. This is important for intending teachers. You need sufficient familiarity with the different ways people perceive things to be able to understand how learners struggle.

What does the feedback cover?

The feedback covers the maths that appears in the audit, and often goes beyond it. In some cases it goes beyond it in content; very often it extends to ideas from other areas of maths. You may have been able to get the answer to a question right to your own satisfaction, but the feedback will be more rigorous. It puts emphasis on correct terminology, which you may not instinctively apply when you look at a question. Accuracy and rigorous examination are important for teachers, who must be able to grasp the meaning of a problem. This ability is particularly important to an understanding of how algebraic structures underpin arithmetic.

What is the content of the feedback?
The feedback refers to each of the eight tasks in the audit. Although the tasks assume that you will have studied maths successfully to a minimum level of GCSE grade C, the feedback offers a different quality of knowing. It goes beyond what you typically need to know to pass an exam.

How should you use the feedback?
You should use the feedback in conjunction with the audit. You should also periodically reread the *Key ideas* section during the course of tackling a question.

How can you make best use of the columns in the feedback?
As in the audit, the two outer columns are intended to help you by providing a quick reference (on the left) and advice and cross references (on the right).

How does the feedback tie in with the Personal learning plan?
You should use the *Personal learning plan* to record and evaluate your progress with the tasks in the audit. As you work through the tasks you will also be referring to the feedback, and as this helps you make links with different mathematical ideas it will form part of your record of progress. Using the feedback to help with the tasks should not be regarded as failure; it is an essential part of developing your knowledge.

How should you follow up the feedback?
Your work on the audit tasks and your notes in the *Personal learning plan* will record your progress. To develop your confidence, return to the tasks from time to time with the purpose of putting more of the connecting ideas into place. Remember that the combination of *Audit*, *Feedback* and *Key ideas* is intended to increase your confidence in maths and your understanding of its special logic and coherence. By completing each task and understanding it fully, you will achieve the mastery that underpins effective teaching and be in a position to take full advantage of the ideas in the second maths book in this series.

Task A: Multiplication and division

This task does not test your recall of number facts such as multiplication tables but addresses the far more important issues of understanding how multiplication and division methods work, the rules underpinning those methods and knowing what answers to expect. So much of what we adults do in mathematics has become instinctive and habitual to the extent that we do not consciously think about why or how we do it. When you do long division you probably do a few jottings and mutter a few well-worn phrases to yourself and, lo and behold, it is done! Now try to explain to a young child what you have done, and why, and that is tricky. After doing the questions in this task you should be more consciously aware of the how and why of some methods and be able to make connections between the various forms of writing numbers.

Read *Key ideas: Keep the value: change the appearance.*

A1

Approximation

(a) Whenever you carry out a calculation you should have a fairly good idea of the size or order of the answer to expect. This is particularly important when using a calculator. Normally the calculation is performed mentally after putting each number to one significant figure. In this case you would do 40×30 and obtain an estimate of 1200.

Long multiplication

(b) Each of the methods shown is a different way of representing the traditional vertical long multiplication algorithm. This algorithm is an efficient method for calculations that are too long or too hard to do mentally. It is best remembered when each step has been understood.

An algorithm is a step-by-step method.

Distributive law

The first method represents the multiplication
$43 \times 27 = 43 \times (20 + 7) = (43 \times 20) + (43 \times 7) = 860 + 301 = 1161$.
This is based on the distributive law for multiplication and addition:

$$k \times (a + b) = ka + kb$$

Commutative law for addition

The second method represents the multiplication $43 \times 27 = 43 \times (7 + 20)$. The only difference between this and the first method is the order in which you multiply the tens and units, and the reason that you can write these either way is based on the commutative law for addition:

$$a + b = b + a \qquad \text{i.e.} \quad 20 + 7 = 7 + 20$$

Commutative law for multiplication

The third and fourth methods are repeats of the first two with the order of multiplication reversed to 27×43. They are based on the commutative law for multiplication:

$$a \times b = b \times a \qquad \text{i.e.} \quad 43 \times 27 = 27 \times 43$$

A2

Distributive law

In this tabular form each step of the multiplication has been entered in a cell of the table. The steps are the results of expanding the brackets when the distributive law is applied to the problem.

You can read more about algebra in *Key ideas: Algebra.*

$$(a + b) \times (c + d) = ac + ad + bc + bd$$

$$43 \times 27 = (40 + 3) \times (20 + 7) = (40 \times 20) + (40 \times 7) + (3 \times 20) + (3 \times 7)$$
$$= \quad 800 \quad + \quad 280 \quad + \quad 60 \quad + \quad 21$$

A3

Each of these questions asks you to consider the size of the answer only because the result of doing the multiplication 43×27 is given.

Standard form

In questions (k) to (n) the numbers are written in what is called *standard form*. This is a universally accepted way of writing large and small numbers often met for the first time when using a calculator. The number is written with the first digit before the decimal point. This number then has to be multiplied by the required power of ten to make it the right size. For example, 116.1 is written as 1.161×10^2 in standard form. Scientific calculators normally give this power of ten on the right-hand side of the display, but some cheap calculators omit the power or give an error sign as soon as the numbers become too large or too small to handle.

Very large and very small numbers are easier to write in standard form.

Working mentally

(a) 1161	(f) 0.01161	(k) 1.161×10^{17}
(b) 116.1	(g) 11610000	(l) 1.161×10^{-1}
(c) 116.1	(h) 1161000	(m) 1.161×10^{-6}
(d) 11.61	(i) $^-11.61$	(n) $1.161 \times 10^{a+b+1}$
(e) 11.61	(j) 1.161	

The digits are always the same. Only their position (place value) has changed.

A4

Applying number to problems in geometry

It is all too easy to assume that 'using and applying' mathematics means applications to everyday life. Some of the most interesting applications of number can be found in other areas of mathematics. In this case arithmetic operations are applied to geometric problems. You have to decide which operation to use and which numbers to operate on. You also have to interpret the answer and check that the correct units have been given and that the answer is sensible. Unless a particular context is given, any correct answer is mathematically acceptable because maths can go beyond the real world. However, once you have a context you have to check the size of your answer to see whether it is reasonable.

Read more about this in *Key ideas: The nature of maths*

Volume of a cylinder

(a) The volume of a cylinder is calculated by multiplying the area of cross-section by the perpendicular height.

$$\text{volume of cylinder} = 11610 \text{cm}^3$$

The cylinder has a diameter of about 23cm (work this out from the cross-sectional area) and a height of 27cm.

Volume of a cone

(b) The volume of a cone is a third of the volume of a cylinder.

$$11610 \div 3 = 3870$$
$$\text{so the volume of the cone} = 3870 \text{cm}^3$$

The diameter of the base of this cone is about 23cm and its height is 27cm.

You can check the volume of a cone by making one and filling it with, say, rice. You should need three times as much rice for the cylinder.

Volume of a pyramid

(c) The volume of a pyramid is a third of the volume of a prism with a cross-section identical to the base of the pyramid. The volume of such a prism in this case would be equal to the area of the cross-section times the perpendicular height, and this would be the same as the cylinder in (a). The volume of the pyramid would be the same as the volume of the cone in (b). Its dimensions are similar to the cone.

Looking for clues in the language

A5

When interpreting word problems you have to search for clues to decide what operation is required and which numbers are to be used. In a question, the words 'how many' may imply multiplication or division. In this question, the word 'altogether' confirms that multiplication is required.

The answer to this question can be calculated by working out $430 \times 9 = 3870$ or by recognizing that $430 \times 9 = 43 \times 10 \times 27 \div 3$ and using the previous calculations.

Read more about this in *Key ideas: The language of maths*.

Commutative law

A6

Read the expression $3 + 2$ as 'start with 3 then add 2' and you get the correct answer 5. Read it as 'start with 2 then add 3' and you also get 5. We summarize this by saying that 'addition is commutative'. Now look at $12 \div 3$ – 'start with 12 then divide by 3'. The correct answer is 4. 'Start with 3 then divide by 12' gives a different, incorrect answer. Division is not commutative.

Multiplication is also commutative. Read 3×4 as 'start with 3 and think of four lots of it' and the answer you get is the same as for 'start with 4 and think of three lots of it'. It is very useful that addition and multiplication are commutative. If you know the answer to $3 + 2$ then you also know the answer to $2 + 3$.

See more on using algebra in *Audit: Task C*.

Long division

A7

In parts (a) to (f) the number 1161 has been partitioned in different ways. Part (e) is probably one of the most obvious ways of partitioning 1161, particularly if we want to perform the calculation mentally. In this case, the number 1161 has been partitioned into numbers that are easily recognized as multiples of 27. Parts (a), (b) and (d) are the least helpful because the numbers chosen are not in the 27 times table. Part (c) is essentially the same as the traditional long division algorithm because 1161 has been partitioned into the highest tens multiple of 27 and the highest units multiple of 27.

You can find out more about long division in the book on teaching maths to pupils.

Working mentally

A8

As in the question on multiplication, the answers to all these questions can be deduced from the result of $43 \times 27 = 1161$. All you need to consider is the size of the answer and the different forms for representing numbers.

(a) 27   (d) 43   (g) 4.3
(b) 430   (e) 270   (h) 2.7×10^3
(c) 0.27   (f) 43

Questions like this help you to become mentally agile.

Looking for clues in the language

A9

You should read word problems carefully for clues about the operation(s) required. It is not always immediately obvious that a problem requires division, but certain words and phrases can be connected with this operation.

(a) Each child gets 27 pence. The first trigger telling me to do division is the word 'shared' and the second is the phrase 'how much?'.

Inspect the words for their meaning.

Looking for clues again

(b) There were 129 piles of pennies. The first trigger telling me to do division is the act of putting something into piles and the second is the phrase 'how many?'.

A10

All of the answers to these questions can be calculated from the result $43 \times 27 = 1161$ (with which you should now be very familiar).

Finding the height of a cylinder

(a) In this cylinder the volume is 1161cm³ and the area of cross-section is 129cm²; 129 is three times 43. The height can be calculated by working out $1161 \div 129$ or by recognizing that the answer is a third of the answer to $1161 \div 43$, which is 9. The height is therefore 9cm. The formal working is:

$$V = Ah$$
$$1161 = 129h$$
$$1161 = 43 \times 3 \times h$$
$$27 = 3 \times h$$
$$h = 9$$

This cylinder is fairly squat. The diameter of the circular cross-section is about 13cm compared with its height of 9cm.

Finding the height of a cone

(b) The volume of a cone is equal to a third of the base area (A) times the perpendicular height (h). Using previous results you should be able to work out the height mentally. The formal working is:

$$V = \frac{1}{3}Ah$$
$$387 = \frac{1}{3} \times 43 \times h$$
$$1161 = 43 \times h$$
$$h = 27$$

This cone is tall on a very small base area. The radius of the circular base is between three and four centimetres compared with its height of 27cm.

Finding the area of the base of a pyramid

(c) The volume of this pyramid is 129cm³ and the height is 43cm. Using previous results the area of cross-section can be calculated mentally. The formal working is:

$$V = \frac{1}{3}Ah$$
$$129 = \frac{1}{3} \times A \times 43$$
$$387 = A \times 43$$
$$A = 9$$

This pyramid has a very small base area compared with its height. Working mathematically all answers are possible but in a real-life situation the answer needs to be examined carefully with respect to the context.

A11

Looking for clues again

You have to look for clues to decide which operation is required. In this question you are given the result of finding 'the sum of', and because you know that the things you have added (the lengths of the edges) are equal and that there are twelve of them, you can deduce that you have to perform a division.

$$96 \div 12 = 8$$

Task B: Fractions

Rational numbers

When we count 'one, two, three ...' we are using whole numbers. Think about the number three. It can be written in other ways, for instance, $\frac{6}{2}$, $\frac{24}{8}$. If we write it in the form $\frac{a}{b}$ we are expressing it as a rational number. It has the same value as 3, but a different appearance. Other rational numbers are, for example, $\frac{7}{10}$ and $\frac{1}{5}$. We also call these numbers vulgar fractions. They are vulgar because they are in the most basic form for a fraction. There are other forms. The vulgar fraction $\frac{7}{10}$ can be written as .7 or 0.7. This is a decimal fraction. And the same fraction can be written as a percentage (70%), or a ratio (7:10).

Vulgar fractions

Decimal fractions
Percentages

> See *Key ideas: Keep the value: change the appearance*

Numerator and denominator

The logic is in the language.

When a decimal is expressed in the vulgar form $\frac{a}{b}$ we call a the numerator and b the denominator. These words make sense if you think of the everyday language of money. What denomination are those coins? Ten pence pieces. How many (what number) do you have? Four. We need to know the number (the numeral, the numerator) and the type (the denomination, the value) of the currency we are handling when we use money. A vulgar fraction expresses this sort of information. For example, $\frac{7}{10}$ tells us we are dealing with a particular denomination (tenths) and that the number we have of it is seven.

> An irrational number cannot be expressed as a ratio but it can be expressed as an infinite decimal.

B1

Different forms

	$\frac{1}{5}$	$\frac{7}{3}$	0.3	0.$\dot{3}$	10%	1:4	0.6$\dot{7}$	67%	1:17	0.317
vulgar fraction	✓	✓								
proper fraction	✓									
improper fraction		✓								
decimal fraction			✓	✓			✓			✓
finite decimal fraction			✓							✓
infinite recurring decimal fraction				✓			✓			
percentage					✓			✓		
ratio						✓			✓	

B2

(a) A vulgar fraction can be written in symbols or words. A third can be written as $\frac{1}{3}$, 'a third' or 'one third'. It can also be written in the form of a ratio, decimal fraction, percentage or division – i.e. 1:3, 0.$\dot{3}$, $33\frac{1}{3}$% and 1 ÷ 3. Numbers that are equivalent to a third can also be written in all those forms.

> You need to be fluent in moving between the different forms.

Equivalent value

The following numbers are equivalent in value to a third:

$$\frac{2}{6}, \frac{4}{12}, \text{ three ninths}, 1:3, 1 \div 3$$

Different forms

(b) It is important to be able to interchange these equivalent forms flexibly and fluently. It is useful to be able to move between fractions, decimals and percentages instantly.

vulgar fraction	$\frac{1}{5}$	$\frac{1}{10}$	$\frac{1}{3}$	$\frac{2}{3}$	$\frac{1}{4}$	$\frac{1}{2}$	$\frac{1}{9}$	$\frac{1}{100}$	$\frac{1}{8}$	$\frac{1}{50}$
finite decimal fraction	0.2	0.1			0.25	0.5		0.01	0.125	0.02
infinite recurring decimal fraction			0.$\dot{3}$	0.$\dot{6}$			0.$\dot{1}$			
percentage	20%	10%	$33\frac{1}{3}$%	$66\frac{2}{3}$%	25%	50%	$11\frac{1}{9}$%	1%	12.5%	2%
ratio	1:5	1:10	1:3	2:3	1:4	1:2	1:9	1:100	1:8	1:50

B3

It is tempting to reach for a calculator when comparing fractions, but the result of doing, say, 100 ÷ 399 is a long string of digits after the decimal point. You need a good knowledge of place value to be able to use this for comparison with other numbers. A better strategy would be to say '$\frac{100}{400}$ has exactly the same value as a quarter; if I reduce the 400 to 399 (dividing by a smaller number) the fraction will have a value just a little more than a quarter.'

If the fraction is smaller than a quarter or bigger than two thirds, it is outside the required range.

$\frac{1}{5}$ Compare this fraction with a quarter. The numerator is the same. The denominator is bigger (i.e. divide one by a number bigger than four) so the fraction is smaller than a quarter, and outside the required range.

$\frac{100}{399}$ is inside the required range (as already argued).

$\frac{3}{7} = \frac{12}{28} > \frac{7}{28}\left(=\frac{1}{4}\right)$ and
$\frac{3}{7} = \frac{9}{21} < \frac{14}{21}\left(=\frac{2}{3}\right)$
$\frac{3}{7}$ is therefore inside the required range.

$\frac{200}{301}$ If the denominator had been 300 this would be exactly two thirds. The denominator is just bigger than 300 (divide by a bigger number) so the fraction is just smaller than two thirds, and inside the required range.

$\frac{3}{60}$ can be reduced to one twentieth which is much smaller than a quarter and therefore outside the required range.

These are just some examples of the strategies you may have used. You won't always want to use the same strategy.

B4

Start with the bottom row and work out which fractions you have to add to get the row above. You have to work fluently converting fractions to decimals and vice versa.

When you have performed the operation of addition, convert your answer into a different form.

ratio		220:100		260:100		140:100	
percentage	70%		150%		110%		30%
decimal fraction		0.7		0.8		0.3	
vulgar fraction	$\frac{1}{10}$		$\frac{6}{10}$		$\frac{1}{5}$		$\frac{1}{10}$

B5

The table in this question shows how you can link algebra and arithmetic. The instructions given symbolically are clear and concise.

Try to do these in your head.

a	$\frac{3}{5}$	$\frac{2}{5}$	$3\frac{1}{7}$	$3\frac{1}{7}$
b	$\frac{1}{5}$	$\frac{1}{7}$	$1\frac{4}{7}$	$1\frac{1}{5}$
$a + b$	$\frac{4}{5}$	$\frac{19}{35}$	$4\frac{5}{7}$	$4\frac{12}{35}$
$a - b$	$\frac{2}{5}$	$\frac{9}{35}$	$\frac{11}{7}$	$1\frac{33}{35}$
$a \times b$	$\frac{3}{25}$	$\frac{2}{35}$	$4\frac{46}{49}$	$3\frac{27}{35}$
$a \div b$	3	$\frac{14}{5}$	2	$2\frac{13}{21}$
$b \div a$	$\frac{1}{3}$	$\frac{5}{14}$	$\frac{1}{2}$	$\frac{21}{55}$

Converting fractions to decimals

Recurring decimals

Converting decimals to fractions

Objects and images

B6

(a) The number $\frac{3}{8}$ also represents the operation $3 \div 8$. You perform the operation to convert the fraction to a decimal. The result is 0.375, which is a finite decimal fraction.

Fractions represent the operation of division.

(b) You do the same with this fraction, performing the operation $1 \div 3$ to convert it to a decimal, and this time get 0.3333333 ... The result could go on forever. It is a recurring decimal fraction. If we express two thirds as a decimal we get 0.6666666... also a recurring decimal fraction.

This example shows how using decimal representation can lead to unwanted errors.

Now do the same for three thirds, which you know is equal to a whole one. You get 0.9999999... Why? The number 0.9999999... is very, very close to the number 1. It is the nature of the recurring decimal that it introduces minute errors. In many cases these will not affect the outcome significantly. However, when you want really accurate results it is best to work with the fractional representation of a number. You may find that if you repeat the exercise on a calculator you get the answer 0.6666667 for two thirds and 1 for three thirds because the calculator takes account of the errors.

It is the inherent nature of place value that allows you to use this method.

(c) It is easy to convert the number 0.625 to a vulgar fraction because it is a finite decimal fraction. It stands for 625 thousandths and we can write $\frac{625}{1000} = \frac{5}{8}$, dividing numerator and denominator by 125.

(d) The number 0.161616... , a recurring decimal, presents a different problem. We cannot immediately say that it is so many hundredths or thousandths. However, because two digits keep repeating themselves we can multiply the number by 100 to get 16.161616... (If there were three digits repeated we could multiply by 1000, four digits repeated multiply by 10000 and so on.) Now we can write:

Let a be the vulgar fraction, then

$$a = 0.161616...$$
$$100a = 16.161616$$
$$100a - a = 16$$
$$99a = 16$$
$$a = \frac{16}{99}$$

B7

It is useful in maths to think about dealing with objects and then operating on them. For instance, start with the object 3, perform the operation 'add 4', and you get 7. Seven is the image of 3 when it is subject to the operation 'add 4'. We could express it like this:

$$3 \xrightarrow{\text{add 4}} 7$$
object　　　　　　　　　image

The same idea is used in the diagram in this question. The object is the triangle ABC. It experiences some operation. What operation? The measurements are changed so that it keeps its shape but gets larger. It is an enlargement. More specifically, the operation is 'multiply each length by $\frac{3}{2}$'. The image of $\triangle ABC$ is $\triangle A'B'C'$ (spoken as 'A dashed, B dashed, C dashed').

Mathematical notation may seem hard to grasp but it helps to describe shapes precisely.

(a) $A'B' = 6 \times \frac{3}{2}$ cm $= 9$ cm
　　$B'C' = 3 \times \frac{3}{2}$ cm $= \frac{9}{2}$ cm $= 4.5$ cm

Object and image

Enlargement

Linear scale factor

Area scale factor

Ratio

Order of operations

Multiplication is commutative.

(b) If you now think about △ *A'B'C'* as the object and △ *ABC* as the image you can see that the operation needed here is one that makes the object smaller. Why does the question ask about an enlargement if the object gets smaller? When doing maths we have to be comfortable with the idea of an enlargement with scale factor $\frac{2}{3}$ making something smaller, just as an enlargement with scale factor $\frac{3}{2}$ makes it bigger. The term 'enlargement' is used consistently to mean 'change the proportions but keep the shape'.

> See *Key ideas: The language of maths.*

The question asks for the linear scale factor *x* required to turn a length of 7.5cm into a length of 5cm. i.e. $7.5 \times x = 5$ and $x = 5 \div 7.5 = \frac{2}{3}$.

Notice the relationship:

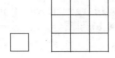

$$\text{object} \xrightarrow{\text{linear scale factor} = \frac{3}{2}} \text{image}$$
$$\triangle ABC \qquad\qquad\qquad \triangle A'B'C'$$
$$\text{image} \xleftarrow{\text{linear scale factor} = \frac{2}{3}} \text{object}$$

> The inverse operation of multiply by $\frac{3}{2}$ is to multiply by $\frac{2}{3}$.

(c) Think about what happens to the area of the shape when we enlarge the lengths. Start by thinking of a square and enlarging it with scale factor of three.

The area increases by a scale factor of 9

> It follows that the volume scale factor is p^3. Check this for yourself.

In general if a shape is enlarged by a linear scale factor of *p* the area is increased by an area scale factor of p^2.

In this question you need to calculate $7.5 \times \frac{3}{2} \times \frac{3}{2} = 16.875$. The area of the enlarged triangle is 16.9cm² (to one decimal place).

(d) The linear scale factor is $\frac{2}{3}$, so the area scale factor is $\frac{4}{9}$.

(e) $A'B' : AB = 7.5 : 5 = 3 : 2$

(f) $A'C' : AC = 6 : 9 = 2 : 3$

(g) (area of △ *A'B'C'*) ÷ (area of △ *ABC*) = 16.875 ÷ 7.5 = 9 ÷ 4 = 2.25

(h) Area of △ *ABC* as a percentage of the area of △ *A'B'C'* = 225%.

(i) $\frac{3}{2} \times \frac{2}{5} = \frac{6}{10}$ and $\frac{5}{2} \times \frac{2}{3} = \frac{10}{6}$. The first represents the linear scale factor of enlargement from △ *ABC* to △ *A"B"C"* and the second represents the inverse enlargement from △ *A"B"C"* to △ *ABC*.

B8

(a) It doesn't matter which way round the waiter works out the final price of the meal. To calculate a 10% discount the amount has to be multiplied by 0.9 (i.e. 100% − 10% = 90% = 0.9). To calculate the 15% service charge the amount has to be multiplied by 1.15 (i.e. 100% + 15% = 115% = 1.15). If we begin with the £84 and multiply first by 0.9 and then by 1.15 we get the same answer as multiplying first by 1.15 and then by 0.9 because multiplication is commutative.

> The different problems on percentages can cause difficulties unless you stop to think what operation you are doing and on what you are operating.

Confusion often arises because we talk about 'adding on a service charge' and 'taking off a discount' when the actual operation in each case is multiplication. We might work out the 15% service charge and then add it on to the amount but these combined operations are equivalent to the single operation of multiplication by 1.15.

Working backwards

(b) If £21 had been collected as a service charge, this was 15% of the cost of the meal (since this was his first visit the customer did not qualify for the 10% loyalty discount). If 15% of something is £21, then 5% is £7 and 100% is £140. You may have said:

Let the cost be x pounds

$$15\% \text{ of } x = £21$$
$$100\% \text{ of } x = £(21 \div 15 \times 100).$$

> Setting the question out algebraically can help you to see how to solve the problem.

B9

Working out the original price

The child has assumed that the 10% applies to the final amount and has added 10% of that final amount to £180. In fact the 10% reduction was on the original and, as yet unknown, price. After a reduction of 10% you know that 90% of the original price is £180. The quickest way of working this out mentally is to say that if 90% is £180 then 10% is £180 ÷ 9 = £20, so 100% was £200.

B10

Looking at what you are operating on

In this question the 10% is operating on a different amount each time. In the January sales the 10% is of a larger amount and so the reduction in the sale is bigger than the pre-Christmas increase. The sale price is lower than the original price.

Let the original price be P. The pre-Christmas price would be $1.1 \times P$. The January sales price would be $0.9 \times (1.1 \times P) = 0.99P$ which is less than P.

B11

Scales on maps

(a) The scale 1:100 000 means that every centimetre on my map represents 100 000 centimetres of land or sea. Now 100 000 centimetres is 1000 metres which is 1 kilometre. So 12.5cm on the map represents 12.5 kilometres.

> Ratio is always expressed so that the two quantities are in the same units.

(b) The scale 1:250 000 means that every centimetre on the map represents 250 000 centimetres of land or sea. Now 250 000 is 2500 metres which is 2.5 kilometres. To work out what 38Km would measure on the map you have to calculate 38 ÷ 2.5 = 15.2.

Gradient

B12

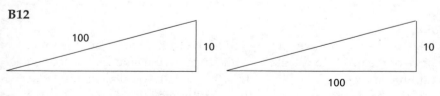

> You could use trigonometry to solve this question but it is simpler to inspect the diagram.

Inspect the two right-angled triangles. In the first instance the distance given as 100 metres is along the road which is the length of the longest side of the triangle, the hypotenuse. The horizontal distance must therefore be less than 100 metres. In the second instance the horizontal distance is equal to 100 metres. The gradient (or steepness) of each triangle is given by the ratio of vertical : horizontal. This ratio will be greater in the first triangle because you are dividing 10 by a smaller number. The first instance therefore indicates the steeper hill, although the difference is very small (only two hundredths of a degree).

Task C: Generalized arithmetic

Number and algebra

Number and algebra are often taught as two unconnected subjects. School pupils learn how to find factors of numbers in the primary school and years later how to factorize algebraic expressions. They are rarely shown how the two are linked.

See *Key ideas: Algebra*.

Using letters

3a means 3 times a

Order of operations

Mathematicians have borrowed the letters of the alphabet to assist them in representing general statements about number. When we see a letter in an algebraic expression such as $3a$ we know that the letter a can stand for any number unless we are given further information that restricts the values it can take. We also know that writing $3a$ means multiply the number a by 3. This is a universally accepted convention. Another convention in arithmetic is that, in the absence of brackets, we perform multiplication and division before addition and subtraction. Brackets can be used to change the order of operations, giving priority to the operations inside the brackets. We need to take great care when we use calculators because some are programmed to operate this algebraic logic whereas others are not.

Check your own calculator to see if it uses algebraic logic.

C1

Multiplication before addition

(a) In the absence of brackets, multiplication and division take precedence over addition and subtraction. The correct order of operations in this expression is first to multiply the 6 by 3, then add the 7. This gives the answer 25.

Calculators are not always correct.

(b) A calculator that does not operate algebraic logic would perform the operations as they are entered. In this case the 7 is added to the 6 to get 13, which is then multiplied by 3 to obtain the incorrect answer of 39. Calculators are not always right!

See that you understand the relationship between the arithmetic and algebra.

Arithmetic conventions apply to algebra.

(c) Fluency in number assists work in algebra. In this algebraic expression the same conventions apply and the multiplication is performed before addition, giving an answer of 29.

C2

Using brackets

Try to be economical with the use of brackets. Do not use them unless you want to change the order of operations. You can save time by inspecting the answer and asking yourself how best to obtain, say, a large negative number. If you try to do this question by trial and error without pausing for thought you could waste precious time.

You may have used more brackets in your answer and still obtained the correct result. This is not wrong but some of your brackets are probably redundant.

(a) $2.2 - 3.3 + 4.4 - (5.5 + 6.6) = {}^-8.8$
(b) $2.2 - 3.3 + 4.4 - 5.5 + 6.6 = 4.4$
(c) $2.2 - (3.3 + 4.4 - 5.5) + 6.6 = 6.6$
(d) $2.2 - (3.3 + 4.4 - 5.5 + 6.6) = {}^-6.6$

C3

Identifying errors

Each answer has been obtained by performing the operations in the order in which they are written rather than by following the correct conventions. This is the most common error that people make, particularly when using a calculator.

The correct answers are: (a) 16 (b) 6 (c) 8 (d) 28

C4

Using a calculator

The inner brackets are not absolutely essential in this calculation because you should always work out multiplication and division before subtraction. Follow the conventions and work out 2 times 6 first (inner brackets), then divide by four to get 3, then subtract 3 from 33 (outer brackets) to get 30, then divide 120 by 30 to get 4. There are many different ways of entering this in a calculator but you need to take great care, particularly if you do not have brackets or your calculator does not use algebraic logic. Try out different ways of obtaining the correct answer. When you are learning to use a calculator for the first time, it is useful to perform calculations that you can do in your head because then you can check your answers.

> If you reserve the calculator for hard calculations you may not realize when you press the wrong keys.

C5

Using letters for numbers

Precise language

First of all you need to specify the letters you are using to stand for any numbers. Then inspect the phrase to decide what needs to be done with the letters. The language associated with maths is very precise and the algebraic expression must convey the exact meaning.

> Read *Key ideas: The nature of maths* and *Key ideas: Algebra*.

Let the two numbers be x and y then

Sum

(a) The sum of two numbers is: $\qquad x + y$

> The word 'sum' is often used to mean 'any arithmetic calculation'.

Difference

(b) The difference between two numbers is: $\qquad x - y$

(The word 'difference' is used to mean various things in maths. Although it normally triggers subtraction, it is often taken to mean 'take the smallest number from the biggest number', particularly in primary schools.)

Product

(c) The product of two numbers is: $\qquad xy$

Quotient

(d) The quotient of two numbers is: $\qquad \dfrac{x}{y}$

Let the number be x then

Square

(e) The square of a number is: $\qquad x^2$

Square root

(f) The square-root of a number is: $\qquad \pm\sqrt{x}$

(We often refer to the square root to indicate the positive square root, but we must remember that the negative value also exists.)

(g) The sum of a number and its square is: $\qquad x + x^2$

C6

When you express a geometric relationship algebraically you are writing a formula to help you work out the value of that relationship for any given dimensions. It is what we call the 'general case'.

> A formula is a helpful aid when doing calculations. Some are used so often that they are worth memorizing.

Area of a rectangle

(a) The area of a rectangle with sides of length x and y is: $\quad xy$

Perimeter of a rectangle

(b) The perimeter of a rectangle with sides of length a and b is:
$$2a + 2b$$

Area of a square

(c) The area of a square with sides of length c is $\qquad c^2$

Area of a triangle

(d) The area of a triangle with base of length b and height h is $\quad \frac{1}{2}bh$

Area of a trapezium

(e) The area of a trapezium with parallel sides of length a and b and perpendicular distance between them h is $\qquad \frac{1}{2}(a + b)h$

Using letters to give instructions

C7

Let n be the number you think of and follow the instructions:

$$\frac{2n+9+n}{3} - 3$$
$$= \frac{3n+9}{3} - 3$$
$$= n + 3 - 3$$
$$= n$$

Make up some of your own to amaze your friends.

Substituting numbers for letters

Working backwards

> Maths can help you make up your own puzzles and games to give you hours of enjoyment.

C8

The first row is straightforward substitution into an algebraic expression. In the rest of the table you have to work backwards to find b and c. You can check your answers to the last two columns by working out $ab + ac$ (adding columns four and five) and $ab - ac$ (subtracting columns four and five).

a	b	c	ab	ac	$a(b + c)$	$a(b - c)$
10	17	3	170	30	200	140
5	3	6	15	30	45	⁻15
8	7	2	56	16	72	40
0.2	0.3	0.5	0.06	0.1	0.16	⁻0.04

Working backwards

C9

Working out the entries to this table is a little more complicated. Not only do you have to work backwards but you may also have to solve equations. For example, in the third row down:

$$2a + b = 17 \quad (1)$$
$$2(a + b) = 20 \quad (2)$$

Multiplying out the brackets in equation (2) gives $\quad 2a + 2b = 20 \quad (3)$
Subtracting equation (1) from equation (3) gives $\quad b = 3$
Substituting in equation (1) gives $\quad a = 7$

> Working backwards often means solving equations.

a	b	a^2	$(a + b)^2$	$2a + b$	$2(a + b)$	$\frac{1}{a}$
5	3	25	64	13	16	0.2
8 ⁻8	⁻6 26	64 64	4 324	10 10	4 36	0.125 ⁻0.125
7	3	49	100	17	20	$\frac{1}{7}$
10	2.5	100	156.25	22.5	25	0.1

Looking for clues

Doing detective work

C10

When we read out an algebraic expression it is easy to assume that the listener knows what we mean. You have to inspect the entries in this table to decide which expression heads which column. You have two pairs of numbers for each expression to help you to decide. The three tables on this page show how maths can be like detective work.

x	$(3x)^2 - 9$	$3x^2 - 9$	$3(x^2 - 9)$
⁻3	72	18	0
⁻2	27	3	⁻15
⁻1	0	⁻6	⁻24
0	⁻9	⁻9	⁻27
1	0	⁻6	⁻24
2	27	3	⁻15
3	72	18	0

C11

Let the number be n where n is an integer.

Even numbers

(a) Any even number is divisible by two, so whatever the value of n, the number $2n$ will always be divisible by 2 ($2n$ has a factor of 2).

Odd numbers

(b) Any odd number is not divisible by two, so by taking any even number and either adding or subtracting one you get an odd number. You can therefore write either $2n + 1$ or $2n - 1$.

Numbers divisible by 7

(c) You can use the same logic to devise a way of writing any number divisible by seven. The expression $7n$ will always be divisible by 7 ($7n$ has a factor of 7).

Square numbers

(d) Any square number is a number multiplied by itself and can be written as $n \times n$ or more elegantly as n^2.

Triangle numbers

(e) Any triangle number is one that belongs to the sequence 1, 3, 6, 10 ... and the general term of this sequence can be written as $\frac{n}{2}(n+1)$.

Cubic numbers

(f) Any cubic number is a number multiplied by itself three times and can be written as $n \times n \times n$ or more elegantly as n^3.

C12

(a) It is useful to know simple rules for divisibility such as 'numbers ending in zero are divisible by 10' or 'numbers ending in zero or five are divisible by 5' and so on. The rule for a three digit number to be divisible by nine is not so well known but it can be useful when we are looking for factors. The rule can be expressed as:

Divisibility by 9

$$\frac{a+b+c}{9}$$

(b) Since three is a factor of nine, the same rule will apply to numbers divisible by 3. You can look for other patterns in your tables. Investigate multiples of 11. What do you notice?

C13

Factors of numbers

(a) The word 'factor' when applied to numbers means 'those whole numbers that divide exactly into the number'.

$18 = 1 \times 18$, $18 = 2 \times 9$, $18 = 3 \times 6$, so the factors of 18 are 1, 2, 3, 6, 9, 18.

Prime factors of numbers

(b) Prime factors are those factors that are also prime. The factors of 20 are 1, 2, 4, 5, 10 and 20, and of these 2 and 5 are prime numbers. We can write $20 = 2 \times 2 \times 5$.

Common factors of numbers

(c) Factors that are common to 45 and 60 are 3, 5, 15.

Highest common factors

(d) First we write each number as a product of its prime factors and inspect each for common prime factors.

$42 = 2 \times 3 \times 7$ $\qquad$ $63 = 3 \times 3 \times 7$ $\qquad$ $98 = 2 \times 7 \times 7$

The highest common factor of all three numbers is 7.

Factors in algebra

(e) Without knowing the value of x, y or z you can write down the factors only from what is given. In algebra the word factor is defined as any number (rather than any whole number) that divides into the number. For example, factors of xyz must be: 1; factors of x, y, and z; x, y, and z themselves; the products in pairs xy, xz, yz; and xyz itself. A number can be written as the product of its factors.

(f) Again, without knowing the values assigned to the letters, you can only write down any common factors from what is given. In this case, 2 is a factor of $2a$ and $2b$. (They are both even numbers.)

Common factors in algebra

(g) In this case, the known common factor of $3ax$ and $5ay$ is a.

(h) The expression $(x-1)(x+2)$ represents a number. Two factors of this number are the numbers $(x-1)$ and $(x+2)$. (Remember that a number can be written as the product of its factors.) Now look at the second algebraic expression and you will see that a common factor is $(x-1)$.

Factorize

(i) The word 'factorize' is an instruction to write the expression as a product of factors. Before you can do that you have to inspect the expression for common factors and take them outside a set of brackets and simplify the expression inside the brackets.

$$(x-1)(x+2) + (x-1)(x-3) = (x-1)(x+2+x-3) = (x-1)(2x-1)$$

C14

Using algebra to do arithmetic

(a) $31^2 = (30+1)^2 = 30^2 + 60 + 1 = 900 + 60 + 1 = 961$

(b) $53^2 = (50+3)^2 = 50^2 + 300 + 9 = 2500 + 300 + 9 = 2809$

(c) $49 \times 51 = (50-1)(50+1) = 50^2 - 1^2 = 2500 - 1 = 2499$

(d) $28 \times 32 = (30-2)(30+2) = 30^2 - 2^2 = 900 - 4 = 896$

> If you practise using these results you can use them to help you with mental arithmetic.

C15

Multiplication is commutative.

(a) True. Let the numbers be a and b, then $a \times b = b \times a$ (the commutative law).

Division is not commutative.

(b) False. Let the numbers be a and b, then $a \div b \neq b \div a$ unless a and b are the same number. More accurately: $a = \pm b$. (Division is not commutative.)

Counter example

(c) False. $a + b \neq ab$. The statement is not true for all numbers. For example $a=2$ and $b=3$ provide a counter example. To find the exceptions, assume the statement to be true.

Let $a + b = ab$ then rearranging $a(1-b) = -b$ and $a = \frac{-b}{1-b}$.

Algebraic convention

(d) True: $(ab)^2 = a^2b^2$ (This is algebraic convention.)

Multiplying brackets

(e) False: $(a+b)^2 \neq a^2 + b^2$ unless a or b are zero, because:

$$(a+b)^2 = (a+b)(a+b) = a^2 + 2ab + b^2$$

> See *Key ideas: The nature of maths* and *Key ideas: Proof.*

C16

Algebra saves time

When you do mathematical investigations you should always look to see if you can express the investigation algebraically because this can save you time later.

(a) Let the length of the rectangle be x and the width be y then for the numerical value of the area to equal the perimeter $xy = 2(x+y)$.

The square as a special case

(b) For a square $\qquad x = y$
$$\text{so } x^2 = 4x$$
$$\text{and } x = 4$$

Task D: Pattern and proof

Exploring in mathematics

Exploring in mathematics often results in a sequence of numbers that fit a pattern. You need to be able to describe those patterns and find other members of the sequence. There are many strategies for this that can save you time and energy. It can be exhausting to keep trying different examples but you can often get results and prove them by using algebra. You need to convince yourself that you have sufficient information to provide a foolproof case.

See Key ideas: Proof.

D1

Sequence of odd numbers

(a) 9, 11, 13, 15 are the next four odd numbers.

(b) You can work them out by counting on two each time.

(c) 19 is the tenth odd number.

The *n*th odd number

(d) The *n*th odd number is $2n - 1$ (check for $n = 10$, $20 - 1 = 19$, and this is correct).

The difference between terms

(e) The difference between each successive term is two.

The sum of the odd numbers

(f) The sum of the first odd number is 1, of the first two odd numbers is 4, of the first three odd numbers is 9, and so on. The sum of the first n odd numbers is n^2.

You may have started with $n = 0$ in which case the *n*th term is $2n + 1$.

D2

(a) Some number sequences are given names according to the pattern that can be made by arranging dots (or some concrete materials) in geometrical patterns such as squares or triangles.

Pythagoras and his followers spent much time studying number patterns.

1   3   6

The sequence of triangle numbers

The numbers in this sequence can be represented by an array of dots in the form of triangles.

(b) The next four numbers in the sequence are 15, 21, 28, 36.

(c) For each successive number you add one more than you did previously.

The *n*th triangle number

(d) 55 is the tenth triangle number.

(e) The *n*th triangle number is given by $\frac{n}{2}(n+1)$.

You can read this as 'start with the number of the term, multiply by the next number and halve your answer'.

The difference between terms

(f) The differences between successive terms are the set of counting numbers.

(g) Each number in the sequence 3, 5, 8, 12 is two more than the first four terms of the triangle numbers.

(h) You do not know whether the sequence continues in this way. If it were to do so, the *n*th term would be $\frac{n}{2}(n+1)+2 = \frac{n^2+n+4}{2}$.

It is easy to assume that if you have a few terms of a sequence they are sufficient to define it.

D3

(a) The first five numbers of the sequence are 1, 4, 7, 10, 13 ...

A linear expression

(b) An algebraic expression is linear if it can be represented on Cartesian co-ordinates as a straight line. It can be recognized by noting that the highest power of the variable (in this case n) is one.

The 'power' of a number can also be called its 'index'.

(c) The difference between successive terms is three.

D4

(a) The first five numbers in this sequence are 2, 5, 10, 17, 26 ...

A quadratic expression

(b) An algebraic expression is quadratic if the highest power of the variable is two.

Looking at subsequent differences

(c) The first differences are 3, 5, 7, 9 ... and the second differences are all two. The second differences are all the same for a quadratic expression whereas the first differences are all the same for a linear expression.

(d) It would be logical if the third differences for a cubic were all the same. (Check with the expression n^3.)

> The shape of a quadratic graph is a parabola.

> Knowing about successive differences can be helpful in finding nth terms.

D5

(a) The child has assumed that the sequence continues by doubling each term. The nth term would be 2^n.

(b)

```
        2    4    8   16   31   57
          2    4    8   15   26
            2    4    7   11
              2    3    4
                1    1
```

The fourth differences

A quartic expression

This pattern suggests that the sequence is generated by a quartic expression and if we continue in this way the next two terms would be 99 and 163.

(c) If $5n - 7 = 148$ then $n = 31$, so 148 is the 31st term.

The Fibonacci sequence

(d) Each term is the sum of the previous two terms, so the next five numbers will be 21, 34, 55, 89, 144.

> A quartic expression is one where the highest power of the variable is four.

> Fibonacci was a famous twelfth–thirteenth century Italian mathematician.

D6

(a) Each number is the sum of the two numbers above.

Pascal's triangle

(b) The next three rows are:

```
      1    6   15   20   15    6    1
    1    7   21   35   35   21    7    1
  1    8   28   56   70   56   28    8    1
```

The sum of the rows of Pascal's triangle

(c) The sum of each row is 1, 2, 4, 8, 16, 32, 64, 128, 256 ... The sum of the nth row will be 2^{n-1}

(d) $(a + b)^2 = a^2 + 2ab + b^2$ The coefficients (the numbers in front of the letters) are 1, 2, 1, which is the third row of Pascal's triangle.

> You could try multiplying out $(a + b)^3$ and inspect the coefficients.

D7

```
   1    2    3    4    5    6    7    8    9   10
  10    9    8    7    6    5    4    3    2    1
```

Summing the counting numbers

(a) Each column adds up to eleven.

(b) The sum of the first ten counting numbers will be $11 \times 10 \div 2 = 55$.

(c) The sum of the first n counting numbers will be $n(n + 1) \div 2$.

> See *Key ideas: Proof*.

D8

Squares on a chess board

(a) 4×4 board   1 big, 4 smaller, 9 smaller, 16 smallest.

5×5 board   1 big, 4 smaller, 9 smaller, 16 smaller, 25 smallest.

8×8 board   1, 4, 9, 16, 25, 36, 49, 64 giving a total of 204 squares.

(b) You would add $1^2 + 2^2 + 3^2 + 4^2 + \ldots + n^2$

Using a formula

(c) Substituting 1 then 2 then 3 etc. for n gives 1, 5, 14 ... and so on, which is correct for the total number of squares.

> The logic is in the geometric structure of the problem.

D9

This question shows how there is no need to try lots of different cases when the formula can be argued from the inherent structure of the problem. There can be no doubt of the answer because specific rules are being followed in constructing the pattern.

Arguing from the inherent structure

(a) A row of black tiles requires a row of white tiles either side plus six at the ends, so for 15 black tiles there will be $30 + 6 = 36$ white tiles.

(b) Using the same logic for n black tiles there will be $2n + 6$ white tiles.

Generalizing

(c) The same number of tiles is required top and bottom but now there will be four white tiles either side making a total of $2n + 8$.

(d) The total number of tiles for m rows and n columns is $2m + 2n + 4$.

(e) For each row there are two white tiles and for each column there are two white tiles. Additionally there are four white tiles at each corner.

> If you always remember to pause for thought before doing a maths problem you can save yourself time and energy.

D10

Finding a formula

(a) Let the width of the rectangle be x. Then the length of the rectangle will be $x + 2$.

$$\text{Area of rectangle} = x(x + 2)$$
$$\text{Perimeter of the rectangle} = 2x + 2(x + 2) = 4x + 4 = 4(x + 1)$$

(b) 65Kg is given 5ml, so 1Kg will be given $(5 \div 65)$ml.

80Kg will be given $(80 \times 5 \div 65)$ml, which is approximately 6ml.

Generalizing

(c) For someone weighing nKg give $(n \times 5 \div 65)$ml.

> Finding the value for one unit is called the 'unitary method'.

D11

(a) The customer will have a standard charge of £25. Since 15 minutes of calls are free, you need to work out the cost of 2 hours 20 mins 10 secs of calls. This amounts to 8410 seconds. At a cost of 1 penny per second this amounts to £84.10. The total charge will be £109.10.

Finding a formula

(b) Let n be the total time in seconds. Then the total cost will be £$[(n - 900)x \div 100 + 25]$.

(c) The total cost under this tariff would be £$[nx \div 2 \div 100 + 25]$

These charges would be equal when $(n - 900)x = \dfrac{nx}{2}$

Dividing by x and multiplying by 2 $2n - 1800 = n$

$$n = 1800$$

Comparing tariffs

This means that the cost is the same when the customer uses 30 minutes of calls. If you inspect the two sides of the equation you can see that after 30 minutes of calls the first tariff becomes more expensive. With less than 30 minutes of calls the second tariff becomes more expensive.

> This is by no means a simple task. It is not surprising that most of us are paying too much for certain services.

D12

(a) If a, b, c and d are all positive whole numbers, then we can say that $2a$, $2b$, $2c$, and $2d$ are four even numbers.

Then $2a + 2b + 2c + 2d = 2(a + b + c + d)$

This expression is only divisible by 4 if the number in the bracket – i.e. $(a + b + c + d)$ – is divisible by 2. This will be the case when one of the following conditions applies: (i) all of a, b, c and d are even, (ii) all of a, b, c and d are odd, or (iii) two are odd and two are even.

(b) Taking the block of numbers given $8 + 9 + 15 + 16 = 48$
     Taking another block $3 + 4 + 10 + 11 = 28$
     and another $1 + 2 + 8 + 9 = 20$

All these numbers are divisible by 4. Let n be the first number in the block, then the other numbers are $(n + 1)$, $(n + 7)$, $(n + 8)$. If we add all of these together we get $4n + 16 = 4(n + 4)$, and this expression is divisible by 4.

(c) Substituting the numbers 1, 2, 3, 4 ... into the formula gives 11, 13, 17, 23 ... and these are all prime numbers. It would be easy to jump to the conclusion that all such numbers would be prime. If you continue to substitute 5, 6, 7, etc. you will eventually discover a counter example when you get to 11. If you inspect the formula you will see that the number 11 when substituted is a factor of each term, so the result cannot be prime.

> Make sure that you can follow this argument. You may need to discuss it with your tutor.

> You need only one counter argument to disprove a conjecture.

D13

(a) Any quadrilateral ABCD can be divided into two triangles. Since the sum of the interior angles of each triangle is 180°, the sum of the interior angles of the quadrilateral is twice as big and equal to 360°.

> This is not the only way to prove this important result.

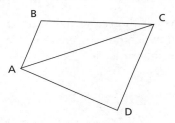

(b) Any pentagon EFGHI can be divided into three triangles. Using the same argument, the sum of the interior angles of a pentagon is three times that of a triangle and is equal to 540°.

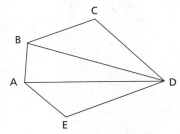

(c) If you continue this argument further you will see that the angle sum is always two less than the number of edges times 180°. This can be written as follows:

The angle sum for an n-sided polygon $= (n - 2) \times 180°$

Side margin labels:

Any even number is divisible by 2.

Stating all possible outcomes

Using algebra to prove a conjecture

Finding a counter example

Proof by deduction

Task E: Equations and graphs

The equals sign in an equation is an indication of balance. Whatever you do to one side of an equation you must do the same to the other to keep it in balance. When you are asked to solve an equation you may be looking for a single solution or a set of solutions. It is easy to state a single solution but a set of solutions may best be illustrated in a graph. When information is presented in graphical form you can study the graph to find the relationship. The shape of a graph, its steepness and points that it passes through, give you the clues to work out that relationship.

See *Key ideas: Algebra* for a discussion of graphical representation of solutions.

E1

(a) $7x = 1484$
   $x = 212$

(b) $2x + 3 = 15$
   $x = 6$

(c) $5x + 130 = 300$
   $x = 34$

(d) $x^2 = 40$
   $x = 6.32$

(e) $x + 5 = 2x - 3$
   $x = 8$

(f) $\frac{x}{4} = 0.5$
   $x = 2$

(g) $\frac{36}{x} = 8$
   $x = 4.5$

(h) $x + y = 10$
   Show solutions as a graph.

(i) $x - y = 2$
   Show solutions as a graph.

Use a calculator.

....

E2

Linear graph

(a) The graph of equations of this type is a straight line. It is a linear (*line*-ar) graph.

Linear equation and linear graph

We recognize equations which give straight line graphs by the fact that they consist of terms in which the power is one. So $y = 3x + 2$ is linear but $y = 3x^2 + 2$ is not linear, nor is $xy = 2$.

(b)

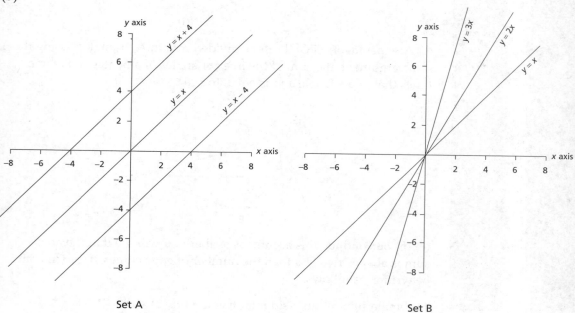

Set A   Set B

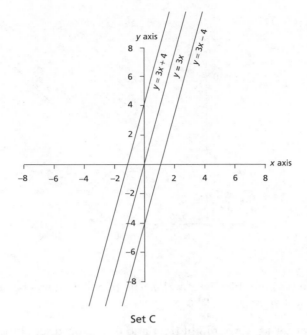

Set C

y = mx + c

(c) Each of the equations is a particular case of the general form of a linear equation: $y = mx + c$. The equation $y = 3x + 2$ is of this form, with $m = 3$ and $c = 2$. The equation $y = x$ is of the same form, with $m = 1$ and $c = 0$.

When we inspect the graphs we see that m tells us how steep the graph is and c tells us where the graph cuts the y axis. In technical language we say that m is the gradient and c is the intercept on the y axis.

E3

Gradient

(a) The graph has a gradient of $\frac{9}{5}$. It cuts the y axis at 32.

(b) This table shows fairly accurate values, but your estimate from the graph could not be this accurate. You may have answers within a few degrees of these.

C	0	100	37	27	35
F	32	212	98.4	80	97

(c)

C	0	100	37	27	35
	freezing point of water	boiling point of water	human blood temperature	hot English summer's day	comfortable bath water
F	32	212	98.4	80	97

(d) To change Celsius to Fahrenheit: write down the number of Celsius degrees; multiply that number by 9; divide your answer by 5; add 32. The result is the equivalent Fahrenheit temperature.

To change Fahrenheit to Celsius: write down the number of Fahrenheit degrees; subtract 32; multiply your answer by 5; divide by 9. The result is the equivalent temperature in Celsius.

Graph of inequality

(e) All the points in the shaded region represent pairs of temperatures (a Celsius temperature and a Fahrenheit temperature). Each pair has a Fahrenheit temperature which is hotter than the Celsius temperature.

E4

(a)

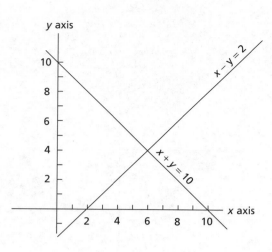

(b) (6, 4)

Solution by inspection

(c) Let the two numbers be x and y. The two statements become:
$x + y = 7$ and $xy = 12$.

Looking at $x + y = 7$ we might try 1 and 6. The product of these is 6. Not enough. Try 2 and 5. Product is 10. Try again. The sum of 3 and 4 is 7; the product is 12. There are two solutions: (3, 4) and (4, 3).

Graphical representation of simultaneous equations

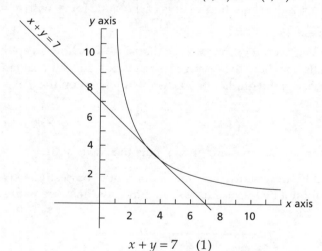

Algebraic solution of simultaneous equations

(d)
$$x + y = 7 \quad (1)$$
$$xy = 12 \quad (2)$$

See *Key ideas: Algebra* for a discussion of variables.

From equation (1) we obtain $\quad y = 7 - x$.
Substitute in equation (2): $\quad x(7 - x) = 12$
$$7x - x^2 = 12$$
$$0 = x^2 - 7x + 12$$
$$0 = (x - 3)(x - 4)$$
$$\text{Either } x = 3$$
$$\text{or } x = 4$$

Substitute in equation (1): when $x = 3$, $y = 4$ and when $x = 4$, $y = 3$. We have two results: (3, 4) and (4, 3). These can be seen on the graph where the curve cuts the x axis.

....

E5

(a)

x	0	1	2	3	4	5	6	7
y	0	25	40	45	40	25	0	⁻35

(b)

maximum height achieved	45 metres
time to reach maximum height	3 seconds
duration of flight	6 seconds
height after 2 seconds	40 metres
height after 6 seconds	0 metres

(c) If we think of the stone being thrown upwards from ground level, the flight after 6 seconds is below ground level (the height is negative). This could be interpreted as continuing its flight into an open mine-shaft. Or it could be thought of as how the stone would continue if it had not already crashed into the ground.

(d) The height at a time of ¯1 seconds is ¯35 metres. This suggests that 1 second before the stone was thrown it was 35 metres below the point where it started. If the experiment started at ground level, the stone was 35 metres underground 1 second before it was thrown. What the mathematical result is suggesting is that if the stone were to be thought of as flying in a continuous trajectory (unhampered by bothersome impediments like the Earth), then 1 second before we took any notice it could be thought of as 35 metres below our observation point.

See *Key ideas: The nature of maths* for a discussion of imaginary worlds.

E6
(b) The table represents an object starting at a height of 90 metres, falling to a height of 45 metres and then climbing again to a height of 90 metres. The graph paints the same picture. What interpretation could we put on this? It could be thought of as a model aeroplane swooping down and up again. But notice that the graph does not indicate the shape of the flight, it only records the changing height during the flight. It could be that our aeroplane did not swoop but plunged down and then abruptly (and miraculously) immediately climbed again.

E7
(a) Train A travelled 200Km from London to Bristol in just under 3 hours without stopping. The train remained at its destination for about 30 minutes and then returned to London without stopping, a journey lasting about 1 hour 30 minutes.

(b) Train B started in Bristol at the same time that train A left London. It travelled for 1 hour, covering 50Km, stopped for half an hour, then travelled a further 50Km, taking 2 hours to do so. After this it stopped again, this time for 30 minutes, before continuing its journey. It reached London 6 hours after leaving Bristol.

(c) The trains passed each other going in opposite directions after about 2 hours 5 minutes. Train A overtook train B on the journey towards London some 4 hours 10 minutes after both began their journeys.

Task F: Geometry

Doing detective work

Doing geometry can be like doing detective work. You inspect diagrams and interrogate words to find clues. Solving problems requires you to be systematic and rigorous. You have to stand back and reflect on your work. You have to ask yourself whether perhaps you need to add another line, or turn a shape around, or ... Then, having solved one step, and another, you find that the whole solution falls into place.

See *Key ideas: The nature of maths.*

Technical words for angles

F1

Technical words like these help to convey mathematical properties in words rather than sentences.

You can refer to 180° as a 'straight-line angle'.

(a) right angle (an angle of exactly 90°)
(b) acute angle (an angle <90°)
(c) obtuse angle (an angle >90° and <180°)
(d) reflex angle (an angle >180° and <360°)

Angles made by parallel lines

F2

When a line is drawn to intersect a set of parallel lines, it is obvious that there are pairs of equal angles formed. Although this is obvious it is not trivial. It forms the basis of many geometrical proofs.

You may find alternative words used to describe these properties but these are recognized internationally.

Vertically opposite angles

a and b are vertically opposite angles (formed by intersecting straight lines).

Corresponding angles

c and d are corresponding angles (formed by the intersection of a straight line with parallel lines).

Alternate angles

e and f are alternate angles (formed by the intersection of a straight line with parallel lines).

Supplementary angles

g and h are supplementary angles (their sum is 180°).

Complementary angles

i and j are complementary angles (their sum is 90°).

Identifying positional relationships

F3

(a) In this question angles are identified by the lines forming them. For example, angle APT is the angle formed by the lines AP and TP. It is the angle at P (the middle letter). Unless otherwise stated, this refers to the acute, obtuse or right angle formed by the lines, and not the reflex angle.

In some cases there are two angles with the specified positional relationship, as in the supplementary angles. However, although angles HTF and TRS have a sum of 90° they are not complementary because first you have to argue that angles HTF and PTQ are vertically opposite.

Angle	$\hat{APT}$	$\hat{PRS}$	$\hat{HTF}$
corresponding	$\hat{CRP}$	$\hat{TPQ}$	
alternate		$\hat{APR}$	
vertically opposite	$\hat{RPQ}$	$\hat{CRE}$	$\hat{PTQ}$
supplementary	$\hat{APR}$ $\hat{TPQ}$	$\hat{CRP}$ $\hat{ERS}$	$\hat{PTH}$ $\hat{FTQ}$
complementary		$\hat{RTS}$	

Using angle relationships to calculate the size of angles

(b) There are several ways of working out the size of the angles required, but you should be able to give a reason for each step. For example:

angle APT = 119°	given
angle TPQ = 61°	supplementary angles APT and TPQ
angle PTQ = 29°	complementary angles TPQ and PTQ
angle CRP = 119°	corresponding angles CRP and APT
angle ERS = 119°	vertically opposite angles

> You should always pause to consider whether you can justify the steps you take.

Similar triangles

(c) Triangle PTQ and triangle RTS are similar. Their corresponding angles are equal (check this).

> This is the only condition necessary to define similar triangles.

Ratio

(d)

SQ:QT = 1:3	given
RP:PT = 1:3	AB is parallel to CD
SQ:ST = 1:4	Q divides the line ST into 1 part and 3 parts giving a total of 4 parts for the whole line of which SQ is one.

> See *Audit: Task B* for more on ratio.

(e) Since SQ:ST = 1:4 then SQ is a quarter of the length of the line ST so SQ = 5cm.

F4

When you do constructions using a ruler and pair of compasses it is important to use a very sharp pencil and to make the arcs clear. Although we tend to learn these constructions by looking at the small part of the arcs that we need to draw, they are all related to the properties of circles. The property of a circle that we use most often is that it has a constant radius. Try drawing the whole circle to see why your construction works.

Constructions using a ruler and a pair of compasses

> Hold the compass at its vertex to avoid changing the radius during a construction.

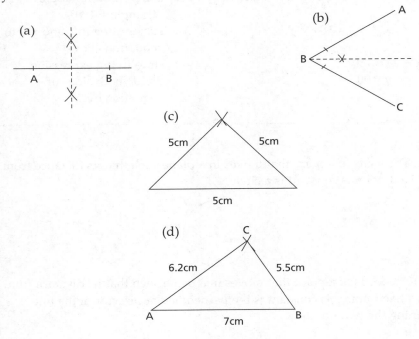

Constructing triangles

(e) If one edge of a triangle is 10cm, the sum of the lengths of the other two edges must be greater than 10cm. For example, if you try to draw a triangle using a pair of compasses with edges 10cm, 5cm and 4cm, the arcs will not meet.

F5

The sum of the interior angles of a triangle

The sum of the interior angles of a triangle is an important result that is used in many other geometric proofs. The proof depends upon a knowledge of angle relationships formed by parallel lines. You do not have to memorize this proof but you should be able to follow its reasoning.

See *Key ideas: Proof.*

Giving reasons

Construction: produce AC to D; draw CE parallel to AB.
Proof:

x = angle BAC = angle ECD   corresponding angles
y = angle ABC = angle BCE   alternate angles
z = angle ACB
$x + y + z$ = BAC + ABC + ACB
          = ECD + BCE + ACB
But ECD + BCE + ACB = 180   angles on a straight line
∴ $x + y + z = 180$

F6

Angles in a semi-circle

You may need to draw some more diagrams to convince yourself that angles in a semi-circle are right angles before studying the formal proof which follows. This is not the only way to prove this result.

Giving reasons

In the circle O is the centre and AC is a diameter.
OA = OB = OC   all are radii of the circle
angle OBA = angle OAB = x base angles of isosceles
                                triangle OAB

angle OBC = angle OCB = y base angles of isosceles
                                triangle OCB

angle ABC = $x + y$ angle ABO + angle OBC
angle OAB + angle ABC + angle BCA = 180   sum of interior angles of a
                                triangle = 180°

$x + (x + y) + y = 180$ substituting in x and y into
                                equation above

$2x + 2y = 180$ simplifying expression
∴ $x + y = 90$ divide both sides of
                           equation by 2

F7

Locus

(a) The locus of a point that moves in a plane such that its distance from a fixed point is constant is a circle.

This reminds us that the radius of a circle is constant.

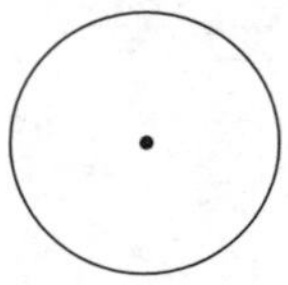

Distance from a fixed point constant

(b) The locus of a point that moves in a plane such that its distance from two fixed points is constant is the perpendicular bisector of the line joining the two points.

Distance from two fixed points constant

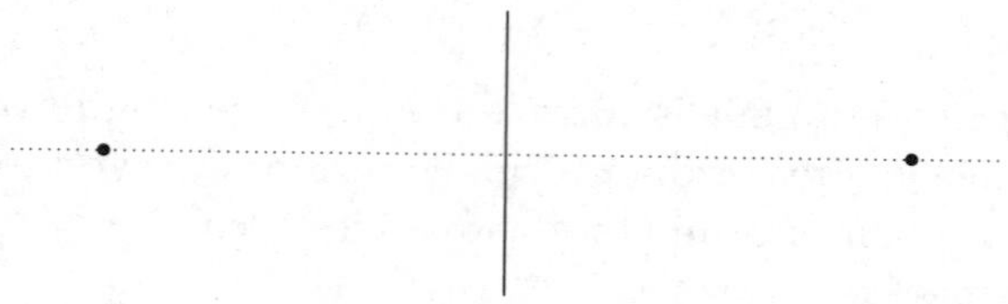

Using and applying maths

(c)

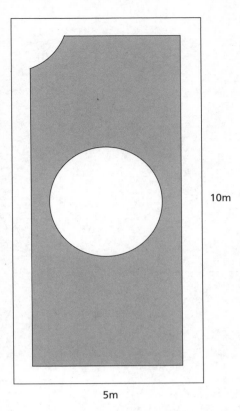

10m

5m

The idea of locus can be applied to many problems in real life.

....

Construct perpendicular bisectors of the lines joining the object and image.

F8

(a) Join two corresponding points on the object and its image. Construct the perpendicular bisectors of each of the lines drawn. The centre of rotation is where these two perpendicular bisectors intersect.

Finding the centre of rotation by trial and error can be exhausting. This method is quicker and more accurate.

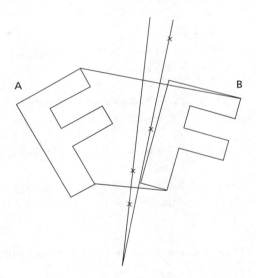

Construct the line perpendicular to the mirror line from the vertices of the triangle.

(b) From each vertex of the triangle construct the line perpendicular to the mirror line. To do this put your compass point at a vertex of the triangle and, with radius greater than the distance from the mirror line, draw arcs on the mirror line. Put your compass point successively at the points where the arcs cross the mirror line and, keeping the radius unchanged, draw intersecting arcs on the opposite side of the mirror line. Join the vertex to this intersection. Use your compass to mark the point on this line equal in distance from the mirror line as the vertex on the opposite side. Now repeat for the other vertices.

Don't be tempted to cut corners by drawing perpendiculars by eye.

Transformations on
Cartesian co-ordinates

This subject can be
extended by studying
matrices and
transformations.

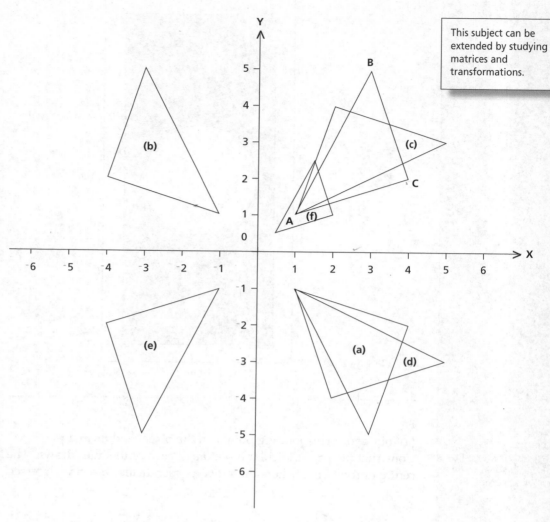

Reflection in the *x*-axis

(a) Reflecting in the *x*-axis: *x* co-ordinates stay the same,
y co-ordinates change sign. Congruent.

Reflection in the *y*-axis

(b) Reflecting in the *y*-axis: *y* co-ordinates stay the same,
x co-ordinates change sign. Congruent.

Reflection in *y* = *x*

(c) Reflecting in line *y* = *x*: *x* and *y* co-ordinates swap over. Congruent.

90° rotation clockwise

(d) Rotating 90° clockwise: the *x* co-ordinate changes sign and becomes
the *y* co-ordinate; the *y* co-ordinate becomes the *x* co-ordinate.
Congruent.

180° rotation

(e) Rotating 180°: both co-ordinates change sign. Congruent.

(f) Enlarging, centring the origin, linear scale factor 0.5:
both co-ordinates are halved. Not congruent (but they are similar).

Task G: Properties of shapes

Words to describe shapes

Properties of a square

Other names for a square

The logic is in the language

Eight triangles on a 3 x 3 grid

Twelve quadrilaterals on a 3 x 3 grid

Area of triangles

When you want to describe a shape to someone, you have many words at your disposal. Each word conveys precise properties. Sometimes you have a choice of words. Take the word 'square' for example. You know that this is a two-dimensional shape that has four straight edges. You know that all the edges are equal, that the shape has four right angles, that opposite edges are parallel and that the diagonals are equal in length and intersect at right angles. All that in one word! The properties of a square mean that it can also be called a quadrilateral (it has four straight edges), a trapezium (it has two opposite edges parallel), a parallelogram (it has two pairs of equal and parallel edges) and a rectangle (it has four right angles). The logic is in the language, and knowing that language can help us to describe and explain in concise ways.

See *Key ideas: The language of maths.*

G1

(a)

Note that you cannot draw an equilateral triangle using this grid. Why?

(i) right-angled isosceles (ii) right-angled scalene (iii) right-angled isosceles (iv) right-angled isosceles

(v) acute-angled isosceles (vi) acute-angled isosceles (vii) acute-angled scalene (viii) acute-angled scalene

(b)

Work systematically to identify all the different quadrilaterals.

(i) square (ii) rectangle (iii) square (iv) parallelogram

  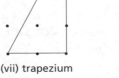

(v) parallelogram (vi) trapezium (vii) trapezium (viii) irregular quadrilateral

(ix) square (x) kite (xi) irregular quadrilateral (xii) trapezium

(d) Area of triangles

Inspect the diagrams for right-angled triangles.

(i)	2cm²	(ii)	1cm²	(iii)	0.5cm²	(iv)	1cm²
(v)	2cm²	(vi)	1.5cm²	(vii)	0.5cm²	(viii)	1cm²

Area of quadrilaterals

Area of quadrilaterals

(i) $4cm^2$	(ii) $2cm^2$	(iii) $1cm^2$	(iv) $1cm^2$
(v) $2cm^2$	(vi) $1.5cm^2$	(vii) $3cm^2$	(viii) $2cm^2$
(ix) $2cm^2$	(x) $2cm^2$	(xi) $2cm^2$	(xii) $1.5cm^2$

G2

(a) In this list, once the properties of a shape have been defined the name of the shape is used to indicate those properties in subsequent definitions.

> The various special cases of a quadrilateral have been given their own names.

Quadrilateral

Quadrilateral: a two-dimensional closed plane shape with four straight edges.

Parallelogram

Parallelogram: a quadrilateral with two pairs of equal and parallel edges and opposite angles equal.

Rhombus

Rhombus: a parallelogram with four equal edges and diagonals that intersect at right angles.

Rectangle

Rectangle: a parallelogram with four right angles and diagonals that are equal in length.

Square

Square: a rectangle with four equal edges and diagonals that intersect at right angles.

Trapezium

Trapezium: a quadrilateral with one pair of opposite edges parallel.

(b) 'All squares are rectangles' is a true statement. Rectangles are quadrilaterals with four right angles. Squares are quadrilaterals with four right angles, so it follows that squares are rectangles. The additional property that squares have is four equal edges. This does not prevent squares from being rectangles but it does make them a special case of rectangle.

> See *Key ideas: The language of maths.*

A square as a special case of a rectangle

'Squares, rectangles and rhombi are all parallelograms' is a true statement. They are all quadrilaterals with two pairs of equal and parallel edges.

Trapezia are not rectangles but rectangles are trapezia.

'All trapezia are rectangles' is a false statement. Rectangles have four right angles, and only special cases of trapezia have this property. It would be true to say that some trapezia are rectangles.

> A shape can have more than the required properties but not less.

'All parallelograms have two lines of symmetry' is a false statement. Some parallelograms do, such as rectangles and rhombi, but they are special cases.

Tessellations using quadrilaterals

(c) Quadrilaterals can be used to draw tessellations because the interior angles have a sum of 360°, which means there will not be any overlap or any gaps when they are placed in order around a point.

Tessellations using regular polygons

(d) The only *regular* polygons that can be used to draw a tessellation are the equilateral triangle, square and regular hexagon. In each case, the size of the interior angle is a factor of 360°.

> You can design many irregular polygons to draw tessellations but these are the only regular polygons you can use.

G3

(a) These measurements can only be approximate because that is the nature of measurement. The circumference should be a bit more than three times the diameter ($C = \pi d$). You can check the results by multiplying the diameter by three and looking to see that the circumference is a bit more than that. If the measurement seems wrong, check by using a better approximation for π, such as 3.14.

Tin A: OK
Tin B: The circumference is too small. It should be more than 22cm.
Tin C: OK
Tin D: The circumference is too big. It should be about 29cm.
Tin E: OK
Tin F: The circumference is too small. It should be about 17cm.
Tin G: The circumference is too small. It should be about 13cm.

(b) The label for such a tin will be a rectangle with length equal to the circumference of the tin and width equal to the height of the tin. The circumference of the tin can be calculated using the formula $C = \pi d$, but first you have to decide which approximation to use for π. You cannot use 3 as an approximation because the label will be too small. You will have to use a better approximation, such as 3.14, but this will give an answer with decimal places that you cannot physically measure. You will have to work to these decimal places whilst working mathematically, then decide the closest measurement that it is practically feasible to use.

Using the approximation 3.14 for π, C= 28.26cm. If you round this to 28.3cm the label should just fit.

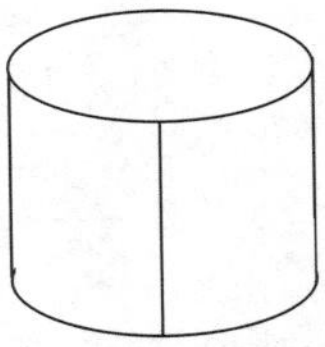

(c) The point p represents a circle with diameter 2.5cm and circumference about 7.9cm. This could be the cross-section of a small cylinder, such as a coin, a tin of modelling paint or a water pipe.

The point q represents a circle with a diameter of 6cm and a circumference of about 19cm. This could be the cross-section of a small tin of soup or a large badge.

The point r represents a circle with a diameter of 10cm and a circumference of 31cm. This could be the cross-section of a tin of beans or a waste pipe.

The point s represents a circle with a diameter of 14cm and a circumference of about 44cm. This could be the cross-section of a tin of paint or a round table mat.

The point t represents a circle with diameter ⁻2 and circumference about ⁻6. We can talk about this mathematically but we cannot find an object in the real world for this to represent.

G4

The perimeter of this figure is 12.56cm.

The area of this shape is 9.42cm².

Left margin labels:

The nature of measurement

Different approximations for *pi*

Deciding which approximation for *pi* is most appropriate

Working mathematically

Using your imagination

Perimeter and area

Right margin notes:

Using 3 as an approximation for π is fine if you are not too worried about accuracy. A better approximation would be 3.14 or 3.142 or the value for π stored in a scientific calculator.

You work to a higher degree of accuracy until you get to the end of the problem.

See *Key ideas: The nature of maths.*

G5

When you think about which boxes to tick, you have to consider how each of the shapes (a) to (h) might satisfy the properties of the shapes in the table. Let's look in detail at (a). The word 'polygon' is your clue for this shape to be a closed plane in 2-D. Its four equal sides tell you that it is a quadrilateral and that it is regular. Its diagonals being equal and intersecting at right angles confirm that it must be a square. These clues also tell you that the sides are parallel and that the shape must have four right angles. So, although the shape is specifically a square, it is also a parallelogram and a rectangle.

> The diagonals of a quadrilateral provide crucial information.

Shape	a	b	c	d	e	f	g	h
2-D	✓	✓				✓	✓	✓
3-D			✓	✓	✓			
regular	✓					✓		
quadrilateral	✓	✓				✓	✓	
parallelogram	✓	✓				✓		
rectangle	✓					✓		
square	✓							
rhombus								
pentagon						✓		
cuboid				✓				
cube								
prism			✓	✓				
pyramid					✓			

G6

(a)

> Test this with more examples of parallelograms with base *a* and height *h*.

In parallelogram EFGH, remove the triangle by cutting along the dotted line and reposition it on the line FG to make a rectangle identical to ABCD. The two areas can be seen to be equal.

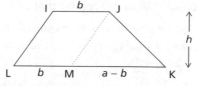

> To calculate the area of a complex shape imagine how it is composed of simpler shapes.

(b) Area of parallelogram IJML $= bh$

Area of triangle JKM $= \frac{1}{2}(a-b)h$

Area of trapezium $= bh + \frac{1}{2}(a-b)h$

$$= \frac{1}{2}(2b+a-b)h = \frac{1}{2}(b+a)h$$

G7

(a) Volume of cube $= (5 \times 5 \times 5)\text{cm}^3 = 125\text{cm}^3$

Volume of cylindrical plug $= (3.14 \times 2.5^2 \times 5)\text{cm}^3 = 98.125\text{cm}^3$

Volume of wood wasted $= 26.875\text{cm}^3$

> Calculate the percentage wasted by dividing the volume wasted by the volume of the cube.

(b) Percentage of wood wasted is 21.5%

G8

Volume of prism = Area of cross-section × height

height = Volume ÷ Area of cross-section

= (1000 ÷ 93.53)cm

= 10.69cm (working to 2 decimal places)

To make this container you would want to ensure that it could hold the contents, so take the height to be 10.7cm.

(a) To get the area of cross-section, you can divide the hexagon into six identical equilateral triangles. The height of each triangle can be calculated using Pythagoras' theorem $h^2 = 6^2 - 3^2 = 27$. Take the square root of 27 to get the height. Work out the area of one triangle and multiply by six to get the area of the hexagon.

(b) The base of the container is the hexagon with area 93.53cm². The sides are six rectangles with length 10.7cm and width 6cm, giving an area of 385.2cm². Total area of plastic = 478.73cm².

G9

If you try different triangles you will find that the equilateral triangle has the greatest area. If you then try quadrilaterals you will find that the square has the largest area for quadrilaterals and that it is also larger in area than an equilateral triangle. Regular polygons give the largest area, and as you increase the number of their edges their area increases. You may have made the conjecture that, using 100cm of string, the polygon with the greatest area you can make is a regular polygon with the most sides you can draw. As the number of sides increases, this shape begins to look more and more like a circle.

The graph below illustrates how the area of regular polygons increases as the number of their sides increases.

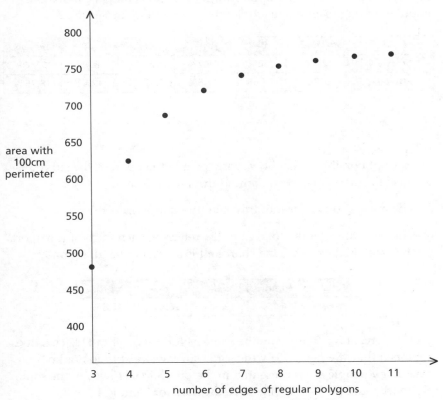

area with 100cm perimeter

number of edges of regular polygons

Sidebar (left margin):

Volume of a prism

Using Pythagoras' theorem

Area of a regular hexagon

Regular polygons have maximum area with a fixed perimeter.

As the number of edges increase the area increases.

Sidebar (right margin):

Having completed the mathematical calculation you have to interpret your answer in the real world.

You can save yourself time and effort by working out a formula for the area of any regular polygon.

See how the area tends towards that of a circle with circumference 100cm (i.e. approximately 796cm²).

Task H: Statistics and probability

A world rich in data

Interpretation of data

The rules of statistics

Summary statistics

Comparing data

Interpreting a pie chart

We live in a world that is rich in data. What does this mean? It means we have available to us a massive amount of figures and pictures and diagrams that relate to the world we live in. Could we therefore say that we live in a world that is rich in information? Not necessarily. The data does not become information until we can see how it relates to the world. We have to undertake some kind of interpretation of the data before we can call it information. Statistics deals with data and information. You are good at statistics when you have a 'feel' for the story behind figures and diagrams. This task is about the rules of statistics; the feedback clarifies what it means to have a 'feel' for the story behind figures and diagrams.

See *Key ideas: The nature of maths.*

H1

(a)

(b) Data sets A and B differ only in the sample size.

(c) Data sets A and C have the same sample size but in every other statistic they are different.

	Data set A	Data set B	Data set C
sample size	11	22	11
smallest	1	1	2
largest	7	7	14
mean	3.36	3.36	6.72
median	3	3	6
mode	3	3	6
upper quartile	5	5	10
lower quartile	2	2	4
range	6	6	12

Calculating and interpreting summary statistics helps to turn data into information.

H2

In both surveys the most popular form of travel is the bus. It is more popular among respondents in Survey 1 than those in Survey 2.

	total no.	bus	train	walk	car	bicycle
Survey 1	2400	50%	16.7%	12.5%	8.4%	12.5%
Survey 2	320	37.5%	12.5%	18.75%	12.5%	18.75%

H3

(a) It is not possible to say how many people took part in the survey because this detail has been omitted from the pie chart.

(b) The most popular form of travel in this sample was the bus.

(c) The percentage of the total sample preferring each form of transport can be estimated from the pie chart and is shown in the diagram.

There are various ways of representing the same information.

bus	train	walk	car	bicycle
50%	16.7%	12.5%	8.4%	12.5%

(d) The percentage figures are the same as for Survey 1 in H2. This does not mean they are necessarily the same survey (we still do not know how many people are represented in the pie chart). However, the same pie chart could be used to illustrate the data for Sample 1.

Comparing data

H4

(a) The clearest information that can be drawn from this data by comparison (without doing any calculations) is: Candidate A received most votes but none of them were from women; Candidate B received votes only from women.

Although you might speculate about Candidate A being sexist and supported by like-minded male voters and Candidate B being a champion of the women's cause, this would only be speculation and is certainly not information that can be determined from the data. Statisticians would not report speculation of this type.

> You can use data to calculate summary statistics but beware of giving an interpretation based on a hunch rather than from the actual evidence.

(b) 240 people voted.

(c) The winning candidate received 50% of the vote.

Working out percentage

(d) 25 % of the members voting at the meeting were women. Notice that we only have data about people who voted: there may have been many more people at the meeting.

(e) A: 0%; B: 66.7%; C: 20%; D: 5%; F: 8.3%.

(f) The pie chart in H3 refers to a survey of forms of travel. It cannot represent the data in H4 because it is marked with the words *car*, *walk*, etc. However, the circle that is cut into sectors (without the words) could be used to represent the total votes cast for each candidate because the figures are the same. The circle would then need to be marked with the words *Candidate A*, etc., and it would become a pie chart.

A frequency table

H5

(a) A frequency table is any table containing data which shows how frequently different events occur. Inspect the completed frequency table shown here. The question 'How frequently was someone with a shoe size of 5 interviewed?' can be answered from the first row: on 8 occasions. The third column, found by multiplying the x value (5) by the frequency of occurrence (8) gives the total shoe sizes of those 8 people. If the data were listed in full, the first column would have 5, 5, 5, 5, 5, 5, 5, 5 and you would add these to get 40. The frequency table makes the calculations tidier.

Survey of shoe sizes of 100 people interviewed in Burnley		
x	f	xf
5	8	40
6	9	54
7	16	112
8	18	144
9	24	216
10	19	190
11	3	33
12	3	36
	$\sum f = 100$	$\sum xf = 825$

Using symbols

The Greek letter Σ (sigma) is used to indicate that specified quantities have to be summed. In the table, $\sum f$ shows that the figures in the f column must be summed. Because f represents the frequency of each shoe size, $\sum f$ is the total frequency (that is, the total size of the sample).

> Greek letters are often used in maths. If you think of sigma as an 's' it helps to remember that it means 'sum'.

The mean, mode and median

(b) Mean, mode and median are shown in the table below.

The mean is calculated by dividing the total shoe size (825) by the total number of people (100).

The mode is found by inspecting the table to see which shoe size occurred most frequently.

The median is found by inspecting the frequency table and using some imagination. Imagine all one hundred people standing in a line with the smallest shoe sizes at one end and the largest at the other end. Walk along the line until you are standing in front of the middle person and read the shoe size of that person. That shoe size is the median. How many people do you count from one end to find the middle person? In reality, there is no person in the middle. Separate them by putting fifty people on your left and fifty on your right and there is a gap in front of you. In maths, you are looking at the $50\frac{1}{2}$th person from either end.

In the data in this sample you can see that, whatever that person looks like, their shoe size must be 8 because both the fiftieth person and the fifty-first person have shoe size eight. To locate this information, look at the f (frequency) column. The first eight people each have shoe size 5, then there are nine people with shoe size 6, which means that number 17 has shoe size 6. Continue this process and you will find that number fifty and number fifty-one both take size 8. The imaginary person number $50\frac{1}{2}$ will also take size 8.

	mean	mode	median
Accrington	8.55	9	9
Burnley	8.25	9	8

Interpreting data

(c) The sample in Accrington and Burnley both have a modal shoe size of 9, although there is a tendency in Burnley for shoe sizes to be smaller: the median and mean in Burnley are lower. Note that we have to be careful in the way we phrase a statistical summary. In this case we cannot even say from the data that Burnley feet tend to be smaller than Accrington feet because it may be that Burnley people like their equally large feet to be more tightly gripped by their shoes!

Interpreting cumulative frequency graphs

H6

(a) The curve shows that the total number of people with shoe sizes less than or equal to 5 is 18; the total number of people with shoe sizes less than or equal to 6 is 47; and so on. The same information appears in the cumulative frequency table. This is the nature of the information in a cumulative frequency table and curve. A cumulative frequency curve often has this distinctive shape. It is known as an ogive. In this case you can see from both the table and the curve that the total number of people with shoe sizes less than or equal to 12 is 400. This is the total size of the sample.

Estimating the median

(b) The median in this sample is the shoe size of the $200\frac{1}{2}$th person. We can estimate from the curve that this shoe size is a little more than 8. We are able to engage in this type of interpretation because we are working in an imaginary world in which shoes are available at any size. This means we can make an estimate which is not restricted by the actual shoe sizes of real life. In this imaginary situation, we can confirm that the median shoe size is a little over 8 rather than very close to 9.

> You have to decide when it is most appropriate to use each average. The word 'average' is often used to convey 'the mean average'.

> Go back and check this with the graph.

> See *Key ideas: The nature of maths*.

Lower and upper quartiles

The lower quartile and the upper quartile are estimated in a similar way. We are looking for the shoe sizes of person number $100\frac{1}{2}$ and person number $300\frac{1}{2}$. An estimate from the curve suggests a lower quartile of a little less than 7 and an upper quartile of a little more than 9.

....

H7

A fair die

(a) The phrase 'a fair die' means a die in which every outcome is equally likely. Although dice can be made with, for instance, twelve faces, we usually assume that a die has six faces labelled from 1 to 6. In this case there are six possible outcomes: 1, 2, 3, 4, 5 or 6. We say that the possibility space is 1, 2, 3, 4, 5, 6. Of all these possibilities, there is just one way of getting a four. The only way we can get a four is to get a four (this is an important way of saying this, even though it sounds a bit silly in this illustrative example). Technically, we say that there is one outcome favourable to the outcome in which we are interested. When the die is fair, the probability P of getting a four, written as P(4), is the ratio of the number of favourable outcomes to the number of possible outcomes. So: $P(4) = \frac{1}{6}$.

> The singular of dice is 'die' but you often hear people call a single die by the name 'dice'.

(b) $P(H) = \frac{1}{2}$.

Equally likely

We have illustrated above that in situations in which each of the possible outcomes is equally likely:

$$\text{Probability of an outcome} = \frac{\text{number of favourable outcomes}}{\text{number of possible outcomes}}$$

When we spin a coin, the size of the possibility space is two (H and T). The number of outcomes favourable to getting an H is one. Asked to calculate P(H), we are seeking to find the probability of getting an H. This is $\frac{1}{2}$.

(c) $P(4, H) = \frac{1}{12}$

Combined events

Asked to calculate P(4, H), we have to find the probability of getting both a 4 and an H. We are dealing with two events combined. We need to think about the possibility space. When we roll a die it is possible to get a 1. If we imagine getting a 1 and then spinning the coin, we have the possibility of getting either an H or a T. So up to this point we can imagine two possibilities for the combined events: (1, H) and (1, T). In a similar way you can imagine (2, H) and (2, T); and so on. It is useful to represent this in picture form.

> You could write out all the possible events to check this result.

coin

T ┤ X   X   X   X   X   X

H ┤ X   X   X   X   X   X
   └─┬───┬───┬───┬───┬───┬── die
     1   2   3   4   5   6

Possibility space

We can now see that the size of the possibility space is 12. We can also see that there is just one favourable event: (4, H). Therefore $P(4, H) = \frac{1}{12}$

> You could also write out all of these events but it would be exhausting. You can see how useful a simple table or diagram can be in maths.

(d) $P(4) = \frac{3}{36}$

We are dealing with two events combined: the rolling of a die followed by the rolling of a die (notice that we can think of it like this even if the two dice are rolled at the same time). We must think about the possibility space. Imagine rolling the first die and getting a 1; when we roll the second die there are 6 possibilities (1, 2, 3, 4, 5, 6). So up to this point we can imagine a possibility space that includes (1, 1); (1, 2); (1, 3); (1, 4); (1, 5); (1, 6). But we have dealt with only one possible outcome for the first die. We can also imagine getting a 2 with the first die, in which case the second die would have the same six possibilities. The complete possibility space is represented in this diagram:

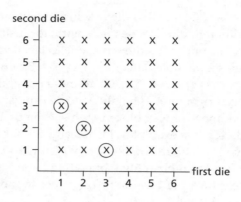

It can be seen that the size of the possibility space is 36. The events favourable to getting a total score of 4 are (1, 3); (2, 2); (3, 1). There are three favourable outcomes. Therefore $P(4) = \frac{3}{36}$.

(e) The discussion above shows how to calculate the probability of combined events by representing the possibility space in a diagram. When we are told that the probability of it raining today is $\frac{4}{10}$, this is an estimate based on meteorological knowledge that, perhaps, a particular cloud formation combined with a certain wind direction at a particular time of year produces rain on a little fewer than half the occasions it occurs. We do not have specific outcomes to deal with as we do when considering dice and coins. The situation in this question is best represented by a tree diagram to show the probabilities, as below:

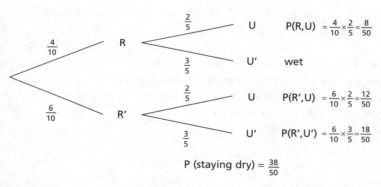

(f) When we deal with very well defined events, like rolling a die or spinning a coin, we calculate the probability of a particular outcome by comparing the number of favourable outcomes with the number of possible outcomes. We can only do this when each outcome is equally likely. In such cases, the calculation of the probability is accurate.

The concept of equally likely outcomes does not apply when dealing with the weather. The use of the idea of probability in these circumstances is just an estimate of how likely something is; it is based on experience or historical data. Once we have put a figure on the probability of an event, we can do calculations in the same way,

Predictions of the weather are based on past statistical evidence. The longer records are kept and the better statistical techniques become the better the prediction.

Experimental evidence

whether we are using accurate 'equally likely events' probability or estimated 'historical data' probability. Our calculations will produce data that we must interpret into information. Our interpretation must take into account what we are dealing with.

(g) This is a mistaken argument. The calculation is wrong and therefore does not support the conviction. The two events, 'life on Mars' and 'not life on Mars', are not equally likely. The probability of life on Mars is not $\frac{1}{2}$.

Equally likely

Events that are not equally likely.

H8

Probability of drawing a court card

(a) $\frac{12}{52}$ is the probability of drawing a court card from the full pack of 52 cards.

$\frac{40}{52}$ is the probability of drawing a card less than eleven from the full pack of 52 cards.

$\frac{11}{51}$ is the probability of drawing a court card from the remaining 51 cards when a court card has already been drawn and not replaced.

$\frac{40}{51}$ is the probability of drawing a card less than eleven from the remaining 51 cards when a court card has already been drawn and not replaced.

$\frac{12}{51}$ is the probability of drawing a court card from the remaining 51 cards when a card less than eleven has already been drawn and not replaced.

$\frac{39}{51}$ is the probability of drawing a card less than eleven from the remaining 51 cards when a card less than eleven has already been drawn and not replaced.

P(C, C) = $\frac{12}{52} \times \frac{11}{51}$ is the probability of drawing a court card followed by a court card.

P(C, L) = $\frac{12}{52} \times \frac{40}{51}$ is the probability of drawing a court card followed by a card less than eleven.

P(L, C) = $\frac{40}{52} \times \frac{12}{51}$ is the probability of drawing a card less than eleven followed by a court card.

P(L, L) = $\frac{40}{52} \times \frac{39}{51}$ is the probability of drawing a card less than eleven followed by a card less than eleven.

Probability of drawing a court card and a number less than 11

(b) The probability of drawing a court card and a number less than eleven (not necessarily in that order) is found by adding P(C, L) and P(L, C):

P(C, L) + P(L, C) = $\frac{480}{2652} + \frac{480}{2652} = \frac{960}{2652} = \frac{480}{1326} = \frac{80}{221}$

It is always best not to reduce fractions in probability questions until the final answer because they are easier to add if they have the same denominator.

Key ideas

The nature of maths

The aesthetic experience of mathematics is perhaps best typified by the spectator's silent moments when poised in the act of apprehending the object rather than remarking on it. Revelation is accompanied by a physiological response, a moment of physical pleasure, that is a distinguishing mark of aesthetic experience. (DUNNE, 1997)

It is difficult to convey the nature of maths.

It is not easy to convey what maths is in a single sentence or paragraph. We want to give you some idea of the nature of maths by talking about the well-known game of noughts and crosses (tick-tack-toe). In this game the criterion for winning is clearly defined: three noughts or crosses in a line. Suppose the winning line is a diagonal from the bottom left corner to the top right corner. We could give you that information in a different way. We could say that the winning line is (1, 1), (2, 2), (3, 3). When we use symbols like this we are beginning to be mathematical. Now think of the game in three dimensions. We could have a winning line that goes from bottom front left to top back right. In symbols this could be given as (1, 1, 1), (2, 2, 2), (3, 3, 3). You could check that this is a winning line by visualizing it, but instead try arguing from the symbols. There are three sets of brackets: that is right because the rules require three in a line. In each bracket there are three numbers where previously there were two: this makes sense because we are in 3D instead of 2D. In each bracket the numbers are the same, showing the same relationship that we see in the 2D version.

> Remind yourself of the game by drawing a diagram and indicating the winning line.

> Now sketch the 3D game and indicate the winning line.

Maths uses symbols.

In this way we become convinced that winning lines can be identified by inspecting the symbols. We need not bother with drawing, making or visualizing the physical representation of the game. We just use symbols. We can now use symbols to play another game. This time a winning line is (1, 1, 1, 1, 1), (2, 2, 2, 2, 2), (3, 3, 3, 3, 3). What kind of game is this? It is five-dimensional noughts and crosses. Do not draw, make or visualize it. Just inspect the symbols. There are three sets of brackets; in each set of brackets there are five numbers; in each set of brackets the numbers are the same. This is a winning line according to the clearly defined criterion for noughts and crosses. Using symbols we have been able to play a game which cannot physically be played. We are playing a game in an imaginary world. This is the nature of maths.

> You cannot draw the 5D game or imagine it without the symbols.

Maths enters imaginary worlds.

You must bear in mind that our discussion of noughts and crosses has been used to *illustrate* what maths is like. It is not an example of what mathematicians do all day. But look carefully at that illustration. Suppose we began to get really involved with this five-dimensional world. We might begin to wonder how many winning lines there are; after all, we have dealt with only one diagonal so far. But our friends would probably shake their heads and worry about why we were not interested in real-life problems. 'You do not understand how *interesting* it is,' we would protest.

To check for winning lines you have to have clearly defined criteria.

Maths is different from science.

This is the nature of maths. It is different from science. Science is an attempt to describe the real world. Science often uses maths: it applies the maths to the real world. It is a bonus that maths can sometimes be useful but this is not the only reason for doing it. Mathematicians do not always refer to the real world. They develop a set of rules that has an internal coherence and logic. They preserve the logic of and make predictions within the system they have created. They work in the imagination. We sometimes say they work in imaginary worlds. Their success in maintaining an internal logic has its reward in an aesthetic experience which means it is *intrinsically interesting*.

Maths has an internal coherence and logic.

The aesthetic experience of maths makes it intrinsically interesting.

It is all too easy to think that the only reason we study maths is because it is useful.

We can summarize the nature of maths as a means of being able to:

A summary of the nature of maths

explore objects in the real world	generate symbols to summarize the real world	use symbols to explore beyond the real-world experience

The way symbols are used is a defining feature of maths.

When we do maths one of the things we do is to use symbols. A defining feature of maths lies in the symbols we use, and the ways we use them (going beyond the real world). But when we use symbols we are not necessarily doing maths. When you are driving and are confronted by the road sign for a cul-de-sac you know that you are entering a cul-de-sac. You are interpreting a symbol but you are not doing maths. Why not? There are two reasons. Firstly, cul-de-sacs are not the sort of objects that mathematicians usually deal with. Secondly, the way in which you are using the symbol does not help you to explore matters beyond the specific cul-de-sac you are faced with. It is useful because it conveys important information but that is all. So, though mathematicians use symbols, this does not mean that every use of symbols is mathematical.

Using symbols in maths is explored more fully in *Key ideas: Algebra*.

Not all symbols are mathematical.

Being numerate is not the same as being mathematical.

Let us use another example to express what maths is and what it is not. We can see people doing maths all the time. Take the case of three children sharing twenty marbles equally among them. When they divide twenty by three and say 'six and two thirds each' they are at that moment being mathematical. When they did the division they were not concerned that two thirds of a marble is useless. When they say 'six each and two left over' they are being numerate but not mathematical. When they say 'six and two thirds each so we'll have six each and leave two in the bag' they are accepting a mathematical result and interpreting it appropriately and they are using and applying mathematics.

When the children decide to use division rather than matching marbles to children they are choosing to be mathematical.

The beauty of maths

The beauty of maths resides in its tendency to provoke speculation. Its essential detachment from the original problem is the key to its power and the basis for the aesthetic experience. The children who use division and contemplate the idea of two thirds before returning to the problem in hand are in a very interesting position. They have a silent moment when they are poised in conscious examination of the real world from a theoretical standpoint. The real world says that two thirds of a marble is useless. The mathematical world says that two thirds of a marble is a valid idea.

Maths takes a theoretical standpoint.

Maths uses symbols. The use of symbols allows and encourages exploration that can take us into imaginary worlds. As mathematicians, we are satisfied when the imaginary world obeys a set of rules even if it does not relate to the world we live in. Another example will help to clarify this.

Select a square piece of paper 10cm by 10cm. Out of each corner cut and remove a square 2cm by 2cm. Fold up the 'flaps' to form a box. The

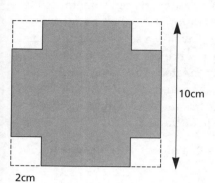

base of the box is 6cm by 6cm. The height of the box is 2cm. Imagine selecting another piece of paper 10cm by 10cm and making a similar box by cutting 3cm by 3cm squares from each corner. The base is ... well, how do we work it out? We started with a length of 10cm and (in our imagination) removed 3cm from one end and 3cm from the other end. After removing this 6cm we have a base left which measures 4cm by 4cm. The 'flaps' are 3cm so the height of the box is 3cm. We are getting a feel for this now. We can make several different boxes. If we imagine cutting corner squares of 1cm by 1cm then we have a box (ten take away one take away one) with a base 8cm by 8cm. The height is just 1cm. If we cut out 4cm by 4cm? No problem. The base is (ten take away four take away four) 2cm by 2cm. The height is 4cm. We can see that from 10cm we remove twice what we cut out from each corner and that gives the size of the square base. The height is just what we cut out. So if we start again with a 10cm by 10cm square and cut from each corner a 6cm by 6cm square we get a base of (ten take away six take away six) ⁻2cm by ⁻2cm. The height is 6cm. So we have a box that measures ⁻2cm by ⁻2cm by 6cm. If we are prepared to think mathematically this causes no problems: we do not object to this imaginary world in which boxes can measure a negative length. On the other hand if we refuse to admit that this world is permitted, then we are not able to work mathematically.

Let us work mathematically. What is the volume of the first box we made? It is 6cm × 6cm × 2cm. The volume is 72cm³. What about the last box we made? Its volume is ⁻2cm × ⁻2cm × 6cm. The volume is 24cm³. Interesting. This box that exists only in our imaginary world has a volume that exists in the real world. Although it is only imaginary it seems to have a very respectable volume of 24cm³. This is the nature of maths.

Our discussion of maths so far has emphasized that it involves using symbols in ways that enable us to work in imaginary worlds (going beyond the information given). This is the nature of algebra, and the discussion is continued as the next key idea. Closely associated with the notion of algebra is another key idea – 'keep the value: change the appearance'. We need to make some reference to this idea now so we will briefly give an indication of what it means. If you think of the number 17 then you can also think of, for instance, (10 + 7), which has the same value (it is worth the same) but looks different (it has a different appearance). This process of keeping the value but changing the appearance is used in different ways throughout maths and

Take a square piece of paper and make the boxes for yourself.

You do not need to make all the boxes. You can start to imagine what they would look like.

Try to imagine what this box would look like.

When you multiply two negative numbers the answer is positive.

This idea is explored more fully in *Key ideas: Keep the value: change the appearance.*

underpins many of the rules we use. You may recall being told that there is not so much to learn in the times tables because if you know 3×7 you also know 7×3. Can you always just reverse the order like this? If you know $7 + 3$ do you automatically know $3 + 7$? Yes: it has the same value but the appearance has changed. When we find examples of this kind of reversal in keeping the value we say that the commutative law is true. So it is true when we add and multiply numbers. But $7 - 3$ and $3 - 7$ do not have the same value; nor do $7 \div 3$ and $3 \div 7$. We say the commutative law is not true for subtraction and division.

> You can find more on the commutative and distributive laws in *Audit: Task A* and *Audit: Task C*.

One of the useful results in maths is that, for instance, $7 \times (40 + 3)$ has the same value as $7 \times 40 + 7 \times 3$. If we calculate 7 times (40 and 3) we get the same value as when we add 7×40 and 7×3. This is true for all numbers. We say that multiplication is distributive over addition. If you make up a few examples you could probably convince yourself that multiplication is also distributive over subtraction.

> Make up some examples with different numbers to convince yourself that this is true for all numbers.

The last section describing the commutative and distributive laws is quite hard to read. You need to persist with it to understand what is being said. It is easier in fact to summarize the commutative and distributive laws in symbols. You will need to inspect these quite carefully and resist any panic, but you will see that algebra offers a concise and elegant way of expressing complicated ideas.

> This idea is explored more fully in *Key ideas: Algebra.*

THE COMMUTATIVE LAW
For all numbers a and b:
$$a \times b = b \times a$$
$$a + b = b + a$$

THE DISTRIBUTIVE LAW
For all numbers a, b, c:
$$a(b + c) = a \times b + a \times c$$
$$a(b - c) = a \times b - a \times c$$

This summary of the two laws is typical of maths. It uses symbols to describe general laws, employing technical language (like 'distributive'). One of the key ideas you are being asked to study is language. We emphasize how the language of maths is helpful in making sense of seemingly complex ideas as long as we are prepared to inspect it, because in maths *the logic is in the language*. We can see this in the word *commutative*. Link this with the everyday idea of a commuter (someone who travels back and forth) and you get a hint about the commutative law. Look at the *distributive* law and see how the *a* is distributed over both the *b* and the *c*.

> This is explored more fully in *Key ideas: The language of maths.*

We have referred to the key ideas of algebra, 'keep the value: change the appearance', and language. Our list of key ideas also includes proof. In order to prove something you have to offer a convincing argument in favour of your case. This sounds like the sort of process that takes place in a court of law, and the court-room comparison is an appropriate one. The person presenting the case has to abide by the rules of evidence and bring enough valid evidence to persuade the jury. In maths, the jury is the group of mathematicians who over the years have built up experience of what is valid. Not all of these people are still alive, and there are so many living ones that it would be impossible to bring them all together. But, just as in the legal system, that knowledge is contained in the laws and rules and books that are studied in order to know the subject.

> This idea is explored more fully in *Key ideas: Proof.*

We have given a brief outline of the first of the key ideas (the nature of maths) and have referred briefly to the others. All of these ideas are closely connected and you will need to read and reread each one to establish for yourself what it means to do maths.

Commutative law

Distributive law

Using symbols to summarize complex ideas

Maths uses technical language.

Maths uses proof.

Algebra

... going beyond the information given. (BRUNER, 1966)

Algebra uses symbols.	One of the things that we do in maths is use symbols. The symbols that we use and the rules and conventions that govern their use are central to maths. This is algebra. It is the language of maths. Algebra enables us to *go beyond the information given*. When we described how to play noughts and crosses we used symbols like (2, 2) in the two-dimensional game and (1, 1, 1) in the three-dimensional version. We were then able to show a winning line in a five-dimensional version. This is a game that we cannot play physically. The symbols allowed us to go beyond the information received through our senses of sight and touch. The symbols enabled us to *go beyond the information given*.
Algebra is the language of maths.	

See the example in *Key ideas: The nature of maths.*

Algebra as generalized arithmetic	In most school maths we learn algebra in relation to arithmetic. In this case symbols (letters) are used to represent numbers. This sometimes causes problems because letters are also used for reasons other than algebra. If we see 'He won the 100m sprint' most of us would correctly interpret the 'm' as 'metres'. This is not algebra: it is an abbreviation.

See *Audit: Task C: Generalized arithmetic.*

Using clues

On the other hand if we see $m + 3 = 7$ there are different clues about the meaning of m. We can see that m is linked to a number by an addition sign. This suggests that m is probably a number (it is certainly not an abbreviation for metres) and it is not difficult to see that in this case $m = 4$. This is the correct answer but we would like you to pretend for a moment that it is not so obvious. We want you to postpone the tendency to grab at the chance to get a right answer and instead follow our thought processes. These will clarify ideas about algebra so that later ideas are readily accessible.

Thinking algebraically

Start again at the point when we noted that m must be a number. Say the words 'I know m stands for all possible numbers. I can look carefully at the clues in $m + 3 = 7$ and see that $m = 4$'. Avoid thinking just '$m = 4$' but think instead 'Of all the numbers that m can be, on this occasion I have sufficient clues to see that $m = 4$'. When you think like this you are seeing m as being a variable rather than just standing for a number.

See *Audit: Task E: Solving equations.*

Using letters as variables

We want to persist with the idea of looking for clues. Look at $x + y = 7$. We can see that two things added together give a number as a result. It is most likely that they are numbers. We must again resist the temptation (often driven by panic) to lurch towards an answer. Say quite deliberately 'x represents all possible numbers and y represents all possible numbers'. Now select from all possible numbers those pairs which, added together, make seven. We might quickly see 1 and 6 or 2 and 5 but the symbols actually invite us to consider every possible pair like 5.2 and 1.8, or ⁻4 and 11, and so on. There are endless possibilities: there is an infinite number of pairs of numbers satisfying this equation.

Going beyond the information given

When doing maths there is always a need to pause for thought.

Looking for additional clues

In the first case ($m + 3 = 7$) we concluded that there is one and only one possible solution ($m = 4$). In the second case ($x + y = 7$) we concluded from the additional clues that an infinite number of solutions exist (we will discuss in a moment how to write them down). The way in which the letters have been used is algebra.

The idea of an infinite number of solutions is discussed in *Key ideas: The nature of maths.*

Being persistent

We must be persistent in looking for clues to help us understand what we need to do. Sometimes in algebra there are clues in the ordinary

Inspecting the clues

language. One example of this is the word 'solve' or the phrase 'find the solutions'. We could, for instance, say 'Solve $x + 3 = 7$' or 'Solve $x + y = 7$' The word 'solve' does not tell us that in the first case there is just one answer and in the second case there is an infinite set of answers. We have to work that out for ourselves by examining the clues. This takes a bit of detective work but it also requires the confidence that comes from experience. That is why we need to practise many examples when we are learning algebra.

Presenting answers

Let's return to our two examples. In the case of $x + 3 = 7$ we can present the answer by writing $x = 4$. In the second case it is not so easy to present the answers to our audience because there is an infinite number of answers. When we are doing maths one of the acceptable ways of presenting the answers is in the form of a graph. Look at graph 1.

> Algebra is not only about using symbols but can also be linked to graphs.

In order to see that the graph does in fact convey the answers we have to look for the clues in the graph itself. To understand this look at graph 2.

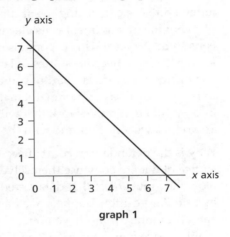

graph 1

Graphical representation

In graph 2, the dot at A indicates the two numbers 2 and 5. This is just one of the infinite set of solutions that we have discussed. B shows another solution: 5 and 2. How did we know that A suggests 2 and 5 and B suggests 5 and 2? We knew because we have learnt the rules of maths.

In graph 2 we have also marked the point C to suggest the solution 6 and 1. Conventionally (according to the rules of maths) we list these three answers as (2, 5), (5, 2), (6, 1). But look now at graph 1. We can see those same suggestions in that diagram. They have not been marked with a large dot, but there is a dot there. Your ability to 'see' the dot is an example of your *going beyond the*

Conventional notation

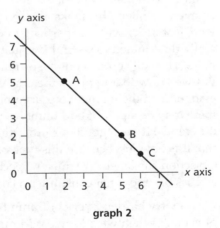

graph 2

Going beyond the information given

information given. There are also dots very close to these three; and other dots very close to those. The straight line can be thought of as made up of all the dots that suggest solutions to $x + y = 7$. Or does it? What about ($^-$12, 19). This is certainly a solution, but is it represented in the graph? Yes it is. When we learn maths we learn that the line that goes to the edge of the picture must be thought of as continuing for ever. We have to imagine all the points implied by the line continuing in both directions. This is another example of maths *going beyond the information given.* People who can interpret graphs in this way are being mathematical because they are using symbols (the graph; the dots implied by the straight line; the pairs of numbers implied by the dots) and *going beyond the information given.* This is the most important purpose of algebra.

> Pause here to imagine the line going to infinity in both directions. Inspect your imaginary line so that you can 'see' all the points.

Proof

PROSECUTING LAWYER: The defendant has a well-known disregard for the law ...
DEFENDING LAWYER: Objection, your honour. My client's high regard for the law is exactly what I intend to prove.
JUDGE: Objection sustained.

Proof is a central feature of the law and of maths. In both professions there are rules which govern what kinds of evidence are admissible and what constitutes a convincing case. These rules are developed from the collective knowledge and experience of the practitioners. When a case is presented the evidence has to conform to the accepted tests of validity or an objection is made and sustained. In both professions the case is judged on how convincing the argument is. One of the typical features of a convincing argument is its elegance and reputations can be made on consistent elegance. This is perhaps not too hard to believe about the legal profession because stories of lawyers' struggles to secure convincing evidence are part of contemporary culture. It may be harder to recognize this as part of mathematics. We want to provide an insight into a mathematician's work that will make this picture more believable. To do this, we will continue with the legal comparison a little longer.

Why is the defendant in court? Because the police have collected sufficient data to convince themselves that they have caught the culprit. Now they must have that data tested formally. Mathematicians are often in a similar position. Suppose we have been looking at even numbers and odd numbers and have noticed that when we add two odd numbers (we may have tried 3 and 7; 9 and 5; 17 and 5) we always get an even number. This looks like an interesting result but perhaps we were just lucky with the particular odd numbers we chose. We feel really determined to see if this is just a freak result. We try another 429 pairs. They all confirm our suspicion and we are feeling really confident. But we know that to prove the case we must have more convincing evidence. At the moment our argument is susceptible to the objection: there may be a pair of odd numbers you have not tried that behave differently. It is no good our protesting that we are really convinced, nor that it is obvious, because this type of evidence is not admissible. Objection sustained. We must respect what kinds of evidence are admissible and what constitutes a convincing case.

We now try harder. Every odd number is the same as 'an even number plus one'. When we add two odd numbers this is the same as 'an even number add an even number add one add one'. This is the same as 'an even number add an even number add two'. This is the same as 'an even number add an even number add an even number' which must be even. Any objections? Are we sure that an odd number is always the same as an even number add one? Yes ... we think so. This seems justified from the fact that odd and even numbers appear alternately (or could this perhaps break down if we kept counting?). Not sure about this. What about the sum of three even numbers coming to an even number. Can we assume this? We are a bit uneasy because this seems to be the same 'level' of problem as the result we are trying to prove. Not sure about this either.

This uncertainty is typical of maths. But as mathematicians we do not give up. We try to construct the same argument more elegantly.

Side notes (left margin):

Proof is central to maths.

A proof is an argued case.

There is a need for elegance.

Admissible evidence and a convincing case

Uncertainty is commonplace.

Search for elegance.

Side notes (right margin):

This is explored further in *Key ideas: The nature of maths.*

Try adding two odd numbers of your choice and check that you always get an even number.

Do you agree that every odd number is an even number plus one?

Key ideas

Let m and n be two positive integers. It follows that $2m$ and $2n$ must be two even numbers because each is divisible by 2. So $2m + 1$ and $2n + 1$ are two odd numbers and the sum of these is $2m + 1 + 2n + 1$ which is the same as $2m + 2n + 2$. This is divisible by 2 because every term is divisible by 2. This means that it is an even number.

2m means two times the integer m. The result of multiplying any integer by two is an even number.

Inviting objections

Any objections? Well ... provided we can accept the premise that $2m$ and $2n$ always represent even numbers and $2m + 1$ and $2n + 1$ odd numbers and that $2m + 2n + 2$ must therefore be an even number then this seems more convincing. In fact it seems pretty watertight. Proof demands the raising of and tussling with these uncertainties. It involves arguing a case. It often employs algebra in order to strengthen the evidence and to increase the elegance of the argument. It is close to our simile of the court case because it involves formal testing of a conjecture about which we are convinced. Proof is a key idea in maths.

Change the appearance of $2m + 2n + 2$ to get $2(m + n + 1)$.

Proof uses algebra to create a strong and elegant case.

Conjectures

Mathematicians may sometimes have an idea which they set up as a conjecture to prove for themselves. Sometimes they spend time working on conjectures made by other mathematicians. One well-known result is as follows: The sum of the first n counting numbers is

$$\frac{n(n+1)}{2}$$

Let us treat this as a conjecture and inspect its elegant proof.

Let the sum of the first n counting numbers be S.
$$S = 1 + 2 + 3 \ldots + (n - 2) + (n - 1) + n$$

Inspect this proof carefully if you are not familiar with it.

We can now write the same expression in reverse order:
$$S = n + (n - 1) + (n - 2) + \ldots + 3 + 2 + 1$$

We now have S written down in two ways (they have a different appearance). If we add S and S we get 2S on the left-hand side and by adding term by term for the right-hand side we get:
$$2S = [n + 1] + [2 + n - 1] + [3 + n - 1] + \ldots + [n - 2 + 3] + [n - 1 + 2] + [n + 1]$$

Notice that our first addition on the right-hand side involves adding n and 1; the second addition involves adding $(n - 1)$ and 2; the last addition involves adding n and 1. When we inspect this we see that:
$$2S = [n + 1] + [n + 1] + [n + 1] + \ldots + [n + 1] + [n + 1] + [n + 1]$$

There is no special significance to the square brackets. It is just a convention.

Now we can see why we changed the appearance of S. When we add the first term and the last term we get $[n + 1]$; when we add the second term and the second from last term we get $[n + 1]$; every time we add a pair of terms we get $[n + 1]$. So we can see $[n + 1]$ written down n times. We have n lots of $[n + 1]$. So:
$$2S = n[n + 1] \text{ and } S = \frac{n(n+1)}{2}$$

This is what we wanted to prove.

Now look back at what we were trying to prove and ask whether you are convinced.

Logical consequence

This is a mathematical argument. It makes clear that one step follows logically from another. It uses algebra to discuss a general case. It is certainly not the only style of mathematical proof but it does have aspects that are worth inspecting. It has a rather pleasing elegance. It is examples of proof like this that enable us to get a feel for what constitutes logic and argument and elegance in maths. It is useful to have learned some examples like this in order to get on the first rungs of the ladder leading to becoming a mathematician. This proof is worth memorizing.

See *Key Idea: Algebra* and *Audit: Task C: Generalized arithmetic.*

A proof worth memorizing

Memorizing a few important proofs will give you confidence.

Keep the value: change the appearance

The dog bit the man. The man was bitten by the dog. The man bit the dog.

The two sentences 'The dog bit the man' and 'The man was bitten by the dog' carry the same information. They look different because the word order has been changed, but it is not just the order of the words. The word 'bit' has been replaced by the words 'was bitten by'. This has been done to make sure that the two sentences carry the same information. If we tried to make up a rule to describe how to change sentences round it would make the process sound very complicated. We would have to make sure that people did not mistakenly write 'The man bit the dog'. This would change the meaning or sense of the phrase. We do not of course do this operation by applying a rule. We know how to do it because we have a lot of experience in using the English language. When we do mathematics we also reorganize mathematical phrases to help us to make sense of them or to make the maths easier to understand or perform. For example, when someone says 'Fifty per cent of a class was absent last Friday' I instinctively think 'Ah! Half of the class was absent last Friday' and if I know that there are thirty children in the class I also think 'That means fifteen children were away last Friday'. Each of these statements looks different (they have changed their appearance), but the sense (the value) has remained. We will describe this sort of change in maths as one in which we 'keep the value: change the appearance'. This is a key idea in maths. Let us explore it further.

Suppose we need to add 27 and 46. Many people do this in their heads by thinking: 20 + 40 + 7 + 6. They are able to rearrange the numbers so that they keep the value but change the appearance. They choose an appearance for the numbers that makes them easier to deal with. This rearrangement is very similar to what we did with the sentence 'The dog bit the man', but rearranging the figures is for most people less instinctive. It is because mathematical rearrangements need to be taught that we use the phrase 'keep the value: change the appearance' as a key idea.

With this key idea in mind we begin to see that we actually do it quite often. Weather forecasters tell us, for instance, that temperatures will reach '20 degrees Celsius, 68 degrees Fahrenheit' because they are aware that some of us prefer one appearance (C) and some of us prefer the other (F). Many people remember their own height in feet and inches but have to put it in metres on official forms. There are also rather subtle uses of 'keep the value: change the appearance'. Recipes sometimes require 500 grams of flour and we interpret it as 1lb. This is not accurate, but in the kitchen this change of appearance has kept the value to the extent that it matters.

This idea, constantly used in everyday life and in elementary arithmetic, is also important throughout maths but is not always fully recognized. When we specifically use the idea in thinking about maths we most often see things in new and clearer ways. If we use it in long division, for instance, we can make sense of operations that have served to mystify generations of students. Use whatever written method you have been taught for long division to do 452 ÷ 3 (even if you can immediately see the answer). Then use the following method.

Reorganize mathematical phrases.

Keep the value: change the appearance.

Changing Celsius to Fahrenheit

Long division

We rearrange such phrases in the English language instinctively.

You will find more on equivalent forms for fractions in *Audit: Task B*.

You may rearrange the numbers in a different way to do this sum.

Can you think of other examples where you 'keep the value: change the appearance'?

See *Audit: Task A* for more on long division.

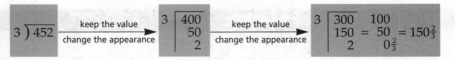

This key idea can also clarify methods of mental calculation. Notice to begin with how the division 36 000 000 ÷ 1 000 000 is straightforward when we think of it as 'How many *millions* make thirty-six *million*? Answer: thirty-six.' When we look at the division 36 000 000 ÷ 1000 it is not especially helpful to think of it as 'How many *thousands* make thirty-six *million*?' But thought of as 'How many *thousands* make thirty-six thousand *thousand*?' it becomes clearer that the answer is thirty-six *thousand*. The idea of replacing thirty-six million with thirty-six thousand thousand is prompted by the key idea of 'keep the value: change the appearance'. With this in mind we can extend the idea to some unusual but very useful changes of appearance. These are some of the ways of keeping the value but changing the appearance of 43 000:

forty-three ten hundreds   four thousand three hundred tens
forty-three hundred tens   four hundred and thirty hundreds

The key idea of 'keep the value: change the appearance' offers a certain flexibility in the way we view numbers. This greater clarity is also apparent in other aspects of maths. We will now look at some geometrical ideas.

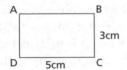 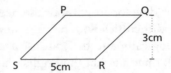

Inspect the rectangle ABCD. Its area is calculated by multiplying the base (5cm) by the height (3cm). The area is 15cm². There is a sense in which this is obvious because we can imagine fifteen squares (1cm by 1cm) drawn inside ABCD and count the area from what we can 'see'. Now inspect the parallelogram PQRS. It is not possible to fit squares inside this in the same way, so calculating the area is more difficult. What we can do is to imagine cutting a triangle from one end of PQRS and sticking it on to the other end.

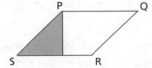 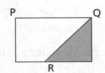

When we do this we *keep the value* of the area *but change its appearance*. Its new appearance is a rectangle the same size as ABCD. We know that rectangle ABCD has an area 15cm² and so parallelogram PQRS also has an area of 15cm². We have been able to calculate this area because we can keep its value while changing its appearance to a shape that is easier to deal with. This process is actually more mathematical than it might seem. When we calculate area we are asking ourselves 'How many squares 1cm by 1cm are needed to fill the shape?' In the real world the answer is that we cannot *fill* parallelogram PQRS with squares. In the imaginary world we can: we need exactly fifteen. This is the nature of maths.

The key idea of 'keep the value: change the appearance' is useful in every aspect of maths. The processes in maths become much clearer when this key idea is kept in mind.

Side labels (left margin):

Reading and speaking numbers

Greater flexibility in mathematical processes

Applying the idea to geometry

Area of a rectangle

Area of a parallelogram

Working mathematically

Side boxes (right margin):

Inspect 43 000 carefully as you speak the words.

Any parallelogram with a base of 5cm and a height of 3cm has an area of 15cm². Sketch some and test this statement for yourself.

This idea is explored further in *Key ideas: The nature of maths*.

The language of maths

The logic is in the language: 'one, two, three ... eleven, twelve, thirteen; one, two, three ... one-ty-one, one-ty-two, one-ty-three ...'

Every profession and every activity has its own technical language. Cooking has its own language. We are told to 'add one tablespoon of sugar'. What is a tablespoon? It is very difficult to find out unless you are working alongside an experienced cook. Does it mean a level one? Oh! *Rounded*. Rounded like this or like this? For the experienced cook the measure *tablespoon* carries information that is invisible to the novice. Learning the technical language takes a good deal of practice.

Maths has its own language. Many of its words are used in everyday language. People sometimes ask 'Do you want the bigger half?' but, technically, 'half' means not only two parts but that they must be the same size. The same size? Do we mean the same length? Or the same volume? Or the same area? Or the same mass? This is beginning to look complicated. But the point about maths is that it has a precise language. In maths we would specify what we are talking about when we cut something in half.

Many words used in maths are borrowed from an everyday language which has developed without the need to be especially accurate. One of the other difficulties with natural language is that it does not always develop logically and this causes problems when it is used as technical language. Imagine that the English language had grown up without any words for counting. You have decided to invent some and you are determined to make it a very logical invention. You start with one set of words – 'one', 'two', 'three', 'four', 'five', six', 'seven', 'eight', 'nine' – then go on to make another. This contains expressions such as 'six-ty', for six lots of ten, and 'seven-ty', for seven lots of ten. You have used '-ty' as an abbreviation for ten – just what English does – but you have continued the logic. You also say that five lots of ten is 'five-ty', and you refer to 'three-ty', 'two-ty' and 'one-ty'. When you teach it to other people they have no difficulty in counting: 'eight, nine, one-ty, one-ty one ... two-ty, two-ty one ... three-ty, three-ty one ...' and so on. The logic is in the language.

The existing written system using figures is logical. We use tens and units, always with the tens on the left and the units on the right. When we speak the numbers we most often read from left to right, as in 64 ('six-ty four'), but sometimes we read from right to left, as in 16 ('six-teen'). In the case of numbers like 16, there is another difference: we do not say '-ty' but '-teen'. There is a good reason for this. 'Six-teen' means six *and* ten; 'six-ty' means six *lots of* ten (six *add* ten and six *times* ten). The logic is in the language but we need pretty good language skills to make sense of it. With alternative counting words like 'one-ty' the logic is much more clearly in the language.

It is because we are so familiar with words in our everyday language that they may act as a barrier to learning when we use them in maths. We sometimes say 'I had a similar experience' when a friend recalls an incident, but in fact our experience is bound to be different. In maths the word 'similar' is used to describe objects that are the same shape although they may be different in size. The trouble is, that definition is

Margin notes (left column)

Maths has its own language.

Many words in maths are borrowed from everyday language.

Words for counting

The logic is in the language.

Reading and speaking numbers

Using familiar words in maths

Margin notes (right column)

You speak the counting numbers instinctively but the construction of the words is not always logical.

Think of other examples of using maths words such as 'average'. Does this refer to the arithmetic mean or the modal value or the median?

Invent your own words for counting so that the logic is in the language.

Eleven and twelve are different again.

Definitions in maths must be precise and sufficiently clear to be used by others.

not good enough for a mathematician. What do we mean by 'same shape'? Is a triangle similar to any other triangle because they both have three sides? No. △ABC (read this as 'triangle ABC')is not similar to △DEF.

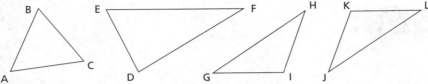

Triangles, and other objects, are similar when corresponding angles are equal and the ratios of corresponding sides are equal. So △GHI is similar to △DEF. Notice that △JKL is similar to △GHI They are similar because ratios of corresponding sides are equal: it does not matter that the ratio is one (which means they are exactly the same size).

When objects are exactly the same size (like △GHI and △JKL) we say they are congruent. We have already said that they are 'similar', but they do not stop being similar because they are congruent. Being congruent is a special case of being similar. This is an important feature of the language of maths: it maintains *continuity* in its meanings. Think of two triangles that are similar but one is much larger than the other. Imagine the larger one getting smaller. Stop. At this point the two triangles are still similar. Continue reducing the size of the one triangle. Stop every now and again. The two triangles are similar. Carry on until the triangle you are changing is smaller than the other triangle. The two triangles are still similar. As mathematicians, we want the process to be continuous so that the triangles are similar at every stage including when they are equal in size. We do not want the discontinuity of saying 'they are similar at each point except when they are congruent'. Our trained instinct as mathematicians is to say that they are always similar and at one point they are congruent as a special case of being similar. We need to appreciate this idea of continuity to see how the logic is in the language.

This instinct for continuity pervades maths. A rectangle is defined as a shape with four right angles.

You can see that ABCD is a rectangle. Look at the square EFGH. Is this a rectangle? Yes. It has four right angles. It does not stop being a rectangle just because it is a square. A square is a special case of a rectangle. Imagine ABCD being stretched so that AB and CD become longer and longer. They get longer than BC and DA. Stop at different points in this process. Is ABCD still a rectangle? Yes, including when AB = BC = CD = DA. This is the instinct for continuity. The tendency in ordinary language is to think of a shape being a square or a rectangle. In maths, we think of a square as being a rectangle.

Maths has its own technical language (and so does cooking). We learn the technical language by using it, working alongside experienced mathematicians who repeat, correct and encourage our own usage. We also need to be tenacious in inspecting written maths in order to identify how the logic is in the language.

Sidebar labels (left margin):

Shapes that are similar

Shapes that are congruent

Continuity in meaning

Continuity pervades maths.

A square is a rectangle.

The logic is in the language.

Sidebar notes (right margin):

The word 'similar' in geometry means that shapes have the same-sized angles and corresponding sides are in the same ratio.

Additional properties do not exclude shapes from particular classifications.

See *Audit: Task G* for more on the classification of shapes.

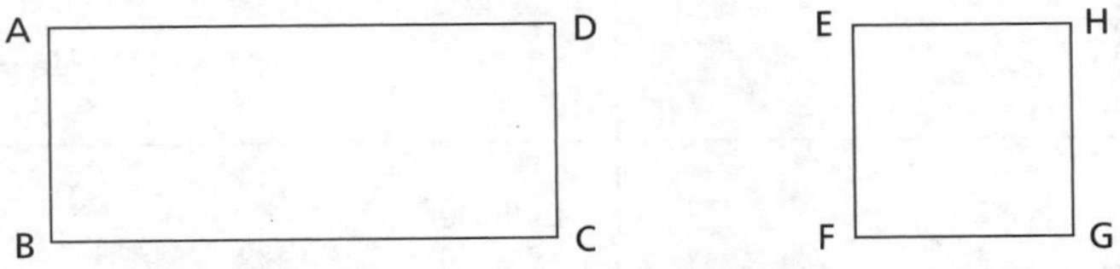

Being a mathematician is a bit like being a detective. You inspect the words to discover the meaning.

Glossary

This glossary is not intended to provide a definition of every mathematical term used in the book. Some of the words and terms are explained fully in the *Feedback* section. We have selected those words, terms and formulae that many people forget but if you are struggling with more than these you can find some excellent dictionaries of maths in libraries, book shops and classrooms. Regular and correct use of mathematical language in the classroom helps children to become familiar with it and to feel more comfortable in its use.

Formulae	
Rectangle Area = ah	**Parallelogram** Area = ah
Trapezium Area = $\frac{1}{2}(a+b)h$	**Triangle** Area = $\frac{1}{2}ah$
Prism Volume = Ah	**Cylinder** Volume = Ah
Pyramid Volume = $\frac{1}{3}Ah$	**Cone** Volume = $\frac{1}{3}Ah$

Term	Definition
algorithm	Any method that is set out in steps that must be carried out in a certain order. You could write an algorithm for getting dressed or making a cup of tea. In maths, algorithms for long multiplication and long division are efficient and effective methods when a calculator is not available.
irrational number	An irrational number is one that cannot be expressed as a ratio, that is, it cannot be expressed as a fraction. It can be expressed as an infinite decimal. Numbers such as π, $\sqrt{2}$, $\sqrt{3}$, e are all irrational numbers.
laws:	The laws below can be expressed in more general terms, but here we are referring to these laws only as they are applied to number operations.
commutative law	The commutative law is very important in arithmetic. It is about the order in which we carry out operations. For example, for addition $3 + 5 = 5 + 3$ but for subtraction $3 - 5 \neq 5 - 3$. The commutative law holds true for addition and multiplication but not for subtraction and division. We can express this law algebraically for any numbers a and b: $a + b = b + a$ $a \times b = b \times a$
distributive law	The distributive law is about the way we combine operations. It is crucial to the algorithms for long multiplication and division and to any method used for mental calculations. We can only partition numbers in certain ways because of this law. We can express this law algebraically for any numbers a, b and c: $a(b + c) = ab + ac$ $a(b - c) = ab - ac$
Pythagoras' theorem	For any right-angled triangle, the lengths of the sides are related in the following way: the square of the hypotenuse is the sum of the square of the other two sides. (The hypotenuse is the longest side of the triangle which is always opposite the right angle.)
tessellation	A tiling pattern where shapes are placed together such that they do not overlap or leave any gaps. We often use the word tessellation to mean a tiling pattern using only one shape.
triangles:	Triangles can be identified by their edge or angle properties:
scalene	all edges are of a different length
isosceles	two edges are equal in length
equilateral	three edges are equal in length
right-angled	contains one right angle
acute-angled	all the interior angles are acute (i.e. less than 90°)
obtuse-angled	one interior angle is obtuse (i.e. between 90° and 180°)

Further reading

This book contains eight tasks in the *Audit* for you to evaluate your knowledge. The *Feedback* section supplies answers and indicates the relationships among different aspects of maths. You may find that you need to do some further reading of basic texts to help you with a particular difficulty. The volume by Dickson *et al* will also prove helpful. The *Key ideas* in the third section offer a framework to help you get a feel for what maths is and what kind of knowledge you need for teaching it. These suggestions for *Further reading* contribute to that wider framework.

Bronowski, J. (1978) *The origins of knowledge and imagination*, London: Yale University Press. This book may seem difficult because there are some rather technical sections. You are advised to persevere even if you cannot make sense of every part. Bronowski provides a vivid picture of science and maths as acts of imagination and discusses knowledge as 'algorithm and metaphor'. He is able to clarify for the general reader why 'there is no way of making mathematical decisions; there are always theorems whose proofs may or may not turn up' (p.77).

Bruner, J.S. (1966) *Toward a theory of instruction*, New York: W.W. Norton & Co. Inc. Many of the themes in this book have received more detailed treatment since its publication. The book nevertheless remains interesting because it brings together a range of ideas and treats them as seriously problematic. Bruner offers powerful insights in single sentences like 'much of perception involves going beyond the information given through reliance on a model of the world of events that makes possible interpolation, extrapolation and prediction'(p.2). He shows how this is relevant to teaching when he discusses the nature of growth, his first point being that 'growth is characterized by increasing independence of response from the immediate nature of the stimulus' (p.5).

Dickson, L., Brown, M. & Gibson, O. (1984) *Children learning maths*, London: Cassell. This book presents 'a review of research in the learning and teaching of mathematics' and is important reading for all teachers. It is not directly relevant to the development of your subject knowledge, but much of the discussion about children's difficulties will be helpful.

Singh, S. (1997) *Fermat's last theorem*, London: Fourth Estate Ltd. '"Since I first met Fermat's last theorem as a child it's been my greatest passion," recalls Andrew Wiles, in a hesitant voice which conveys the emotion he feels about the problem' (p.77). Read this book to understand the passion that mathematicians feel – and to get a unique insight into what mathematics is.

Sobel, D. (1996) *Longitude*, London: Fourth Estate Ltd. 'Precise knowledge of the hour in two different places at once – a longitude prerequisite so easily accessible today from any pair of cheap wristwatches – was utterly unattainable up to and including the era of pendulum clocks (p.5) ... For lack of a practical method of determining latitude, every great captain in the Age of Exploration became lost at sea ...' (p.6). This is the basis of a fascinating story which reveals the nature of scientific endeavour and gives insights into the application of mathematics.

Personal learning plan

The *Personal learning plan is* a way of recording your planning and monitoring your progress. You need to select a task in the *Audit* and begin to work at it. Refer to the *Feedback* and discuss any difficulties with friends and colleagues. You will reach the point where you are confident you understand a piece of work or are certain you need more detailed help. Record either of these stages in the **Initial Record of Progress**.

Suppose you need help. Evaluate your resources. Perhaps the topic is already planned for coverage in your course programme. Make a note of this in the **Action Plan**. It may be that a course tutor offers maths tutorials to respond to individual problems. Should you make an appointment? Whatever you need to do, make a note of it in the action plan so that your intended course of action is clearly set out.

This is good, but the process does not stop there. You need to review your action plan from time to time and check your progress. Make a note of how you are doing in **Update on Progress**.

Below is an example of what your *Personal learning plan* might look like. On the following page are blank templates to help you create your *Personal learning plan*. Start one immediately. Don't put it off or time will pass and you'll not be able to catch up.

Task: A — Multiplication and division

Initial Record of Progress	Action Plan
<u>16 September</u> I can do long multiplication and understand the algorithms. I didn't know the commutative and distributive laws before doing this task but I understand the explanation in the Feedback and in the Key ideas.	Read up on commutative and distributive laws. Long division is being explained in session 4 of maths method class. Talk to maths tutor about language associated with number operations and observe teachers in school. I'm not too good at standard form. I can do division but I do not understand the long division algorithm. I need to work on the language associated with multiplication and division.
	Update on Progress
	<u>13 October.</u> Session 4 excellent. Long division OK. <u>17 October.</u> School-based work good for language — see School Experience file (16th Oct.)

Task:

Initial Record of Progress

Action Plan

Update on Progress

Task:

Initial Record of Progress

Action Plan

Update on Progress